FIRE AND ICE

FIRE & ICE

THE NUCLEAR WINTER

Michael Rowan-Robinson

Longman

Longman Group Limited
Longman House, Burnt Mill, Harlow
Essex CM20 2JE, England
Associated companies throughout the world

© Longman Group Limited 1985

First published 1985

British Library Cataloguing in Publication Data

Rowan-Robinson, Michael
    Fire and ice: the nuclear winter
    1. Nuclear energy—Environmental aspects
    I. Title
    333.79'24   TK9153

ISBN 0 582 44698 8

Set in 11/12½ Apollo "Lasercomp"
Printed in Great Britain by Richard Clay PLC, Bungay, Suffolk

Contents

Preface

Most people do not like to think too closely about the consequences of a nuclear war. This is true whether you are a supporter of a defence policy based on nuclear weapons or, like myself, an opponent. However, I began to be forced to think about these consequences a couple of years ago when my colleague Ian Percival drew my attention to calculations that suggested that a nuclear war would generate a massive cloud of smoke and dust, which could have drastic effects on the earth's climate.

As I have spent the past ten years or so studying (amongst other things) the effects of a cloud of dust around a star on the star's light, I began to think about the rather similar problem of a cloud of dust and smoke surrounding the earth.

After the 1983 Washington conference on 'The World after Nuclear War', at which the findings of the TTAPS group (R.P. Turco, O.B. Toon, T.P. Ackerman, J.B. Pollack and Carl Sagan) and others were announced, the 'nuclear winter' – as it has come to be called – began to enter the public consciousness. The prediction of widespread extinctions amongst plants and animals and the possible extinction of the human species could not be ignored.

There also began to be criticisms of the nuclear

winter calculations. Some of these centred on the uncertainties in estimating how much dust and smoke would be injected into the atmosphere in a nuclear winter and whether it would spread out to shroud the earth. Others doubted whether the nuclear dust and smoke cloud would cause cooling of the earth.

I felt that it would be worthwhile to write a book which explains the nuclear winter effect in simple terms and which discusses where the real uncertainties in the calculations lie. The recently published report by the US National Research Council gives an authoritative discussion of these uncertainties, but still concludes that a strong nuclear winter effect is a real possibility.

I also wanted to discuss the political implications of these calculations. If the nuclear winter prediction stands up to the intense scrutiny it is now receiving (for example a major investigation will be published shortly by the international organisation SCOPE – the Scientific Committee on Problems of the Environment) then there have to be massive reductions in the present nuclear arsenals. But even if the world's scientists were unanimous in recommending this, this would not be sufficient to force the politicians to act. Ultimately the politicians will bow only to widespread and strongly felt public opinion.

I would like to thank Anthony Rudolf for his careful reading of the manuscript. His pamphlet *Byron's Darkness*: *Lost Summer and Nuclear Winter* was a major inspiration during the writing of this book, as also was the series of anti-nuclear pamphlets published by his Menard Press. I would also like to thank my wife Mary for her support and for her many good suggestions.

Some say the world will end in fire
Some say in ice

Robert Frost ('Fire and Ice' 1923)

Chapter 1

To the brink of extinction

The nuclear winter debate

We have all known for years that the consequences of a nuclear war are appalling, unthinkable. Until three years ago, though, we thought that the consequences fell entirely on human beings and mainly on those nations involved in the conflict. An all-out war between NATO and the Warsaw Pact countries would mean the destruction of much of western civilization, with the death of large fractions of the populations of the countries involved and suffering on an un-imaginable scale. It is a remarkable indictment that this prospect alone is not sufficient to force reductions in the nuclear arsenals. We seem to be hypnotized by the fragile peace that has existed in Europe since the Second World War, hoping despite the growing precariousness of our situation that the holocaust will never happen.

However, three years ago a few scientists began to realize that a nuclear war would be a crisis not just for western civilization but for *all* life on the planet. Changes in the earth's climate which have become known as the 'nuclear winter' would have catastrophic biological consequences, with widespread extinctions of plants and animals. Leading biologists are now not able to rule out the possibility that the human species might become extinct. Many scientists from many different fields of study and from many different countries, on both sides of the Iron Curtain, have been drawn into the nuclear winter debate. In this book I shall try to explain the nuclear winter in simple terms and what its consequences are for us all.

Previous dramatic extinction events

One of the most interesting discoveries of the eighteenth and nineteenth centuries was that many species of plants and animals that once flourished on earth are now extinct. The existence of such species is demonstrated by fossils laid down in the earth's geological strata millions, or even thousands of millions, of years ago and was first explained by Darwin's theory of evolution. Darwin believed that species gradually became extinct because they were less well adapted to their environment than their competitors in the continuing struggle for existence. We now realize that there have been several dramatic episodes in which large numbers of species of plants and animals have become extinct over a relatively short time. As the earth is 4600 million years old, geologists and paleontologists tend to think a million years is quite a short time. The most famous of these extinction events occurred 65 million years ago at the end of what is known as the Cretaceous period when the long rule of the dinosaurs on earth came to an end. They had dominated the earth for 200 million years so perhaps can be said to be the most successful animals to have lived on earth so far. The prospects of human beings surviving for 200 million years do not look good at present.

Over the past 700 million years nine great extinction events are known. The earliest known occurred some 650 million years ago, late in what geologists call the Precambrian era, when animal life was still sparse. Many species of acritarch, a type of plankton living in the ocean which consisted of only a single cell, became extinct. Their disappearance coincided with a period when glaciers covered many areas of the earth. Around 530 million years ago the trilobites — crustaceous animals living on the sea-bed — suffered a series of three extinction pulses spread over some 5 million years, each event lasting no more than 5000 years. This was about the time that the earliest fishes evolved. The trilobites were also victims in a mass extinction about 400 million years ago which eliminated some 100 types of marine species, primarily in the tropics. Tropical species were again hard hit by a crisis about 370 million years ago, at the end of the Devonian period. Primitive corals and sponges, builders of limestone reefs earlier in the period, suffered a sudden extinction from which they never fully recovered and many other tropical marine groups disappeared at the same time. This was about the time that vertebrates — animals with backbones — invaded the land for the first time. Other extinctions occurred at the end of the Paleozoic era 250 million years ago and at the end of the Triassic period 140 million years ago when the earliest mammals started to evolve. Then at 65 million years ago the dinosaurs disappeared along with many other plants and animals, though land plants and mammals were little affected. It has been estimated that about half of the species living at that time perished in this extinction. Most recently, at 40 million years ago there was an extinction event which seriously affected, among others, species of plankton and shellfish, and which has been shown to be associated with a severe cooling of the oceans.

What was the cause of these major extinction events? This is still the subject of controversy amongst scientists. The demise of the dinosaurs in particular has attracted many theories to explain it. But there are now two very strong clues to the cause of the extinctions, both of which have a clear relevance to the nuclear winter debate. The first clue is that at two of the extinction events, those of 65 and 370 million years ago, unusually high concentrations of the heavy element iridium have been found. The significance of iridium is that it is normally a rather rare element in the earth's rocks. It is, however, abundant in meteorites, which are believed to be the debris from comets. The concentrations found are more than twenty times greater than is normally found in terrestrial rocks and they are confined to very narrow geological strata, which means that they were deposited over a relatively short period of time. Luis and Walter Alvarez of the University of California, Berkeley, have suggested that the explanation of the iridium concentrations and of the mass extinction events lies in the collision of an asteroid or comet nucleus with the earth.

At this point perhaps I should make an aside on comets, asteroids and meteorites. Comets are large aggregates of rock and ice and most of them reside in a large cloud around the solar system far beyond the orbit of Pluto. A few get deflected into orbits which bring them near the sun (and the earth). When they approach the sun, gases and dust particles are driven out of the head of the comet to give the spectacular tails for which comets are famous. As these comets travel round their elongated orbits, they leave a trail of debris behind them. If the earth runs into this trail, the debris may either burn up as it enters the earth's atmosphere, in which case a meteor or shooting-star is seen, or it may thud to the ground as a meteorite.

Asteroids are irregular lumps of rock ranging in size from one to several hundred miles. Most of them are to be found in a belt between Mars and Jupiter and may be due to a planet that broke up or failed to form. However, some travel on orbits plunging in towards the sun, like the comets, and those that cross the earth's orbit round the sun are called Apollo asteroids. The Apollo asteroids are particularly interesting to us because occasionally one of them actually hits the earth. It is Apollo asteroids which are responsible for the huge craters on the moon. The earth would also be covered with similar large craters were it not for the effects of weathering and the movement of the earth's crust. In 1983 the Infrared Astronomical Satellite, IRAS, discovered a new Apollo asteroid which turned out to have the same orbit as the debris responsible for the Geminid meteor stream. IRAS had therefore proved what had long been believed, that the Apollo asteroids are the heads of comets which have lost all their ice and dust and are therefore no longer capable of generating tails as they approach the sun.

It is these Apollo asteroids or dead comet nuclei which the Alvarezes believe are responsible for the iridium concentrations and dinosaur extinctions of 65 million years ago. Their idea is that an asteroid 6 miles in diameter colliding with the earth would inject sixty times the asteroid's mass as pulverized rock into the atmosphere and that a small fraction of this, perhaps 1000 million tons, would reach the stratosphere, at an altitude of ten miles or more. This dust would remain in the stratosphere for several years and would spread over the whole globe. The resulting darkness would suppress photosynthesis and cause widespread extinctions amongst land plants, plankton, and the animals that feed on them.

The second major clue to the cause of the great extinction events is that in many of them it can be demonstrated that cooling of the oceans played a major role. This is especially true when the extinctions are concentrated amongst tropical marine species, since plants and animals in the tropical oceans have nowhere to migrate to if the oceans cool. Now a dramatic cooling of the earth is one of the consequences of the huge cloud of dust postulated in the Alvarezes' asteroid extinction theory. However Steven Stanley, of Johns Hopkins University, Philadelphia, who has collected together the evidence that ocean cooling is a crucial factor in the major extinction events, argues that several of the species that became extinct at about the time of the dinosaurs' demise 65 million years ago disappeared from the scene well before the iridium layer, which is supposed to mark the impact of the asteroid, was deposited. For other species there is evidence that the extinction was gradual, spread over 2 million years or more. These are problems that have to be resolved before the asteroid extinction theory can be fully accepted. About the reality of the mass extinctions there can be no doubt.

The ice ages

About 10,000 years ago the descendants of a small mouse-like creature that had survived the catastrophe of 65 million years ago, our ancestors, began to emerge from the most recent of the many ice ages that have spread over the earth. These ice ages are brought about by changes of only a few degrees in the average annual temperature of the earth. There have been about ten ice ages in the past million years and they come with a surprising regularity every 100,000 years or so. The most recent one reached its peak about 18,000 years ago and at that time ice sheets covered much of Europe and North America. The amount of ice covering the earth at different times in the past can be estimated by measuring the abundance of isotopes of oxygen in ocean sediments. The normal type of oxygen in water, oxygen-16, has eight protons and eight neutrons in its atomic nucleus. However the oxygen on earth always has a few parts in a thousand of another isotope of oxygen, oxygen-18, with eight protons and ten neutrons in its nucleus. The chemical properties of the two types of oxygen are almost identical, but when water evaporates the slightly heavier form, composed of oxygen-18, tends to be preferentially left behind. When an ice age begins, the ice sheets that form from rain and snow falling on the land tend to have more oxygen-16 than the oceans, which become enriched in oxygen-18. The variations of the oxygen-18 concentration in ocean sediments therefore maps out the history of ice sheet formation. This variation shows some fascinating periodicity, with cycles of ice formation occurring with several different periods of repetition, of 100,000, 43,000, 24,000 and 19,000 years.

These periodicities turn out to have a simple but surprising explanation, which was first put forward by the Yugoslav astronomer Milutin Milankovitch in the first half of this century. As the earth goes round the sun, the variation of the seasons from winter to summer and back again depend on the fact that the axis of the earth's rotation is not exactly perpendicular to the plane of the earth's orbit, but is tilted by about 23.5 degrees. In the northern hemisphere the sun therefore appears higher in the sky in summer and we receive more heat from it. Similarly in winter the sun appears lower in the sky than it would if there were no tilt of the earth's rotation axis and the weather is correspondingly colder. A more subtle contribution to seasonal variations of the amount of heat reaching a given part of the earth is the fact that the earth does not move in an exactly circular orbit, but moves in an ellipse. The degree of flattening of an ellipse is measured by a quantity called the eccentricity. The fact that the earth's orbit is an ellipse, with the sun at one focus, means that there is a point on the orbit where the earth is closest to the sun, called the perihelion. At present this occurs in January each year. Now it turns out that because of the gravitational attractions of the moon and the other planets the tilt of the earth's rotation axis, the eccentricity of the orbit and the time of year of perihelion all vary slowly with time. The eccentricity varies with a period of 100,000 years, the tilt of the rotation axis varies with a period of 40,000 years and the time of perihelion varies in a complicated way with two periods of 23,000 and 19,000 years. Thus the Milankovitch theory explains all the periodicities that are observed in the oxygen-18 abundance and hence in the amount of ice cover. The precise extent of the ice cover is determined by the area over which even the summer temperature remains below freezing point, so that the ice accumulates from year to year.

The ice ages were not as drastic crises for life on earth as those responsible for the massive extinctions we discussed in the previous section. Because the cooling of the earth and the spread of the ice sheets happened slowly, there was time for most species to migrate to find their desired habitats. Even so it has been found that there were significant peaks in the extinction rate at the times of ice ages, especially among tropical species that found themselves trapped in areas like the Caribbean with no warmer place to migrate to.

The great Tambora volcanic eruption and the lost summer of 1816

On 10 and 11 April 1815 the largest volcanic eruption in recorded history took place on the island of Sumbawa, Indonesia. The upper one third of Mount Tambora, which before the eruption was some 14,000 feet high, was blasted into the air with devastating consequences. At least 88,000 people died on Sumbawa and the neighbouring island of Lombok. Rumbling detonations were heard up to 2000 miles away, ash fell up to 1000 miles away and pitch darkness at noon was experienced for the next one or two days at distances of up to 300 miles. Altogether about 100 cubic miles of ash were discharged into the atmosphere. The eruption was about three to ten times more violent than the more famous eruption of Krakatau in Java in 1883.

Although the eruption itself was dramatic enough in its own right, the subsequent consequences over the rest of the globe were in some ways even more dramatic. The eruption column seems to have risen to altitudes of 10 to 20 miles, reaching the zone of the upper atmosphere known as the stratosphere. Small particles of volcanic dust formed a huge cloud which gradually spread round the globe and was to stay up there for two years. The effects of this dust cloud were felt in several ways. Prolonged and brilliantly coloured sunsets and twilights were frequently seen in England during the autumn of 1815. During the spring and summer of 1816, a persistent 'dry fog' was reported in the north-eastern part of the United States, which was not dispersed by surface winds or rain. According to a New York report, this fog reddened and dimmed the sun so much that sunspots became visible to the naked eye. During the eclipse of the moon of 9 and 10 June 1816, observed under clear conditions at Ipswich, London and Dresden, the moon was observed to vanish completely. Normally the moon appears faintly luminous and reddish during an eclipse due to refraction and scattering of sunlight by the earth's atmosphere. Two years after the eruption, on 19 September 1817, while observing an aurora at the Glasgow Observatory 3 hours after sunset, the visiting French astronomer Dupin noticed that the lower part of the sky was inexplicably obscured, despite cloudless conditions, and that stars usually visible to the naked eye could be seen 'only with difficulty'.

The stratospheric dust veil produced by the Tambora eruption had therefore spread from Indonesia, just south of the equator, to Britain within three months. The effects of this dust veil can be measured by the amount by which sunlight was dimmed. Richard Stothers of NASA's Goddard Institute for Space Studies, New York, who has given an excellent account of the Tambora eruption in the magazine *Science*, 15 June 1984, estimates that the peak dimming factor at northern latitudes was to about 25 per cent of normal sunlight, in September 1815. In the summer of 1816, this dimming factor was still to 40 per cent of normal.

There is another way that the amount of material in the Tambora cloud can be measured. It is known that the two main ingredients of volcanic dust veils are silicate ash from pulverized rock and small droplets of sulphuric acid formed from the sulphur ejected from the volcano. Now studies of the Greenland ice cap show that the ice laid down each year can be identified and analysed, rather like the rings in a tree trunk. For the years 1815–18 the Greenland ice shows a much stronger acidity than normal and this is believed to be due to the sulphuric acid from the Tambora cloud as it gradually fell to the ground. The total amount of sulphuric acid in Tambora's stratospheric veil has been estimated in this way to be about 200 million tons and this fits in well with the amount of dimming of sunlight.

The effects of this dust cloud were not just on

observations of the sun, moon and stars. The year 1816
became known in Europe and North America as 'the
year without a summer'. A meteorological record for
New Haven, Connecticut, that had been kept by the
presidents of Yale College since 1779, records June
1816 as the coldest June in that city for 70 years, the
average temperature for the month being some 5 °C (9
°F) colder than normal. Lancashire had its coldest July,
and the summer as a whole ranks as the coldest on
record in the Swiss city of Geneva for the entire period
of 1753 to 1960. Figures supplied by the Swiss
Meteorological Service show that the average temperature for the three months June to August 1816, was
just over 3 °C (5 °F) colder than the average for the same
three months for the hundred years 1761–1810,
1821–1870. In New England the loss of most of the
staple crop of Indian corn and the great reduction of
the hay crop caused so much hardship that the year
became enshrined in folklore as 'Eighteen Hundred
and Froze to Death'. The first of three unseasonable
cold waves moved into New England on 6 June and
lasted till 11 June, leaving 3 to 6 inches of snow on the
ground. Frost struck again on 9 July, 21 August and 30
August. All but the hardiest grains and vegetables
were destroyed. The cold was even more severe in
Canada and even wheat, which had survived in the US,
perished. The Halifax *Weekly Chronicle* noted that
'great distress prevails in many parishes throughout
Quebec Province from a scarcity of food. Bread and
milk is the common food of the poorer classes at this
season of the year; but many of them have no bread.'
The price of wheat and hay soared in North Ameria.
The effects of the poor summer were worse in Europe,

which had just experienced the rigours of the Napoleonic Wars. In Switzerland attempts to replant summer wheat were frustrated by a lack of seed in the state granaries. By the end of the year the shortage of food was severe, particularly in the cities. All kinds of things were eaten: sorrel, moss and cat flesh. Instructions were issued to help people identify poisonous plants. In Poitiers in France rioting broke out because of a tax imposed on wheat. Grain carts on their way to market in towns along the Loire valley had to be protected by soldiers and gendarmes, who found themselves fighting as many as 2000 hungry and enraged citizens. These and other anecdotes are given in a fascinating article by Henry and Elizabeth Stommel in *Scientific American* June 1979.

The 'lost summer' did not go unrecorded in literature. In Geneva during July 1816, was Byron, who had recently left England never to return. While in Geneva, he wrote a remarkable poem, 'Darkness,' which has long been a favourite of mine. It portrays the death of a world plunged into darkness and cold. It is hard not to believe that the poem was inspired by the lost summer during which it was written, as is argued by Anthony Rudolf in his Menard Press pamphlet *'Byron's Darkness: Lost Summer and Nuclear Winter'*. The poem can be read as a chilling forecast of the nuclear winter and begins:

I had a dream, which was not all a dream.
The bright sun was exinguish'd, and the stars
Did wander darkling in the eternal space,
Rayless, and pathless, and the icy earth
Swung blind and blackening in the moonless air;

> Morn came and went – and came, and brought no
> day,
> And men forgot their passion in the dread
> of this their desolation; and all hearts
> Were chill'd into a selfish prayer for light:

Nuclear winter – the new crisis for life on the planet

We have seen that life on earth has faced many crises in which mass extinctions of species ocurred. Today the combination of the high level of human ingenuity and the low level of human wisdom has brought us to the brink of a new crisis. The nuclear arsenals are now so great that a nuclear war between the superpowers would not just bring death and destruction to the combatants and their allies. Dust thrown up by the nuclear explosions and smoke from the widespread fires they cause would create a pall of smoke and dust whose effects would dwarf even those of the Tambora volcanic eruption. Scientists believe that the attenuation of sunlight and the resulting drop in temperature would between them cause the extinction of many species of plants and animals. In the extreme case it is not even clear that the human species would survive.

How did this effect come to be discovered and how was it overlooked for so long? There have been many detailed studies of the consequences of nuclear war. As recently as 1975 a report by the US National Academy of Sciences concluded that there would be no long-term harmful climatological or biological effects of a nuclear war. Then in 1982 Paul Crutzen of the Max-Planck-Institute for Chemistry in Mainz, West

Germany, and John Birks of the University of Colorado in America published the results of a very interesting study in the Swedish environmental magazine *Ambio*. They had set out to examine what damage would be done to the ozone layer at the top of the earth's atmosphere. Ozone is a form of oxygen with three atoms of oxygen instead of the usual two that are found in normal molecular oxygen. The ozone layer plays a crucial role for life on earth by absorbing harmful ultraviolet radiation from the sun. While doing this calculation they decided to estimate how much smoke would be generated in the widespread fires expected in a nuclear war. To their astonishment they found that several hundred million tons of smoke would be injected into the atmosphere and that this would be enough to blot out the sunlight over the whole globe.

Meanwhile another group of scientists had already started to calculate the effects of dust injected into the atmosphere by nuclear explosions. These were: Richard Turco, an atmospheric research scientist and program manager of R and D Associates in Marina de Rey, California; Brian Toon, Thomas Ackerman, and James Pollack, research scientists at NASA's Ames Research Center in California; and Carl Sagan, Director of the Laboratory of Planetary Studies at Cornell University; and they have become known as the TTAPS group from the first initials of their surnames. The group had worked previously on the effects of the dust storms on Mars, which they had had a good view of during the Mariner 9 mission. This spacecraft arrived at Mars in the middle of a spectacular dust storm covering the whole planet. They had next turned their attention to the stratospheric dust veils produced after volcanic eruptions and their effects on the earth's climate. While in the middle of detailed calculations on the effects of dust ejected into the atmosphere in a nuclear war, they heard about the results of Paul Crutzen and John Birks and decided to include the effects of smoke in their calculations. The effects were dramatic, with a serious dimming of sunlight lasting for weeks or months and very large drops in the average temperature on the ground.

In April 1983 about a hundred scientists from the United States and other countries met in Cambridge, Massachusetts, to review the TTAPS group's results and to prepare the ground for a large conference on the effects of nuclear war in Washington later in the year. First a group of physical scientists scrutinized the TTAPS group's report. Then the results were presented to a group of eminent biologists. The biologists' conclusions were startling: the conditions described by the TTAPS group would result in widespread extinctions of plants and animals and the survival of the human species could not be guaranteed.

When the 'World After Nuclear War, the Conference, on the Longterm Worldwide Biological Consequences of Nuclear War' opened on 31 October 1983 in Washington D.C. there were 500 participants plus 100 media representatives in attendance. Participants included scientists and ambassadors or other officials from more than twenty countries as well as public officials, educators, environmentalists, and business, foreign policy and military leaders from throughout the United States. The Conference included a 90-minute television link-up with a panel of distinguished Soviet scientists in Moscow, whose studies supported those of the American scientists. Since that epoch-making Washington conference, many other detailed studies have confirmed the validity of the TTAPS group's calculations and the seriousness of the crisis facing life on earth.

Now we are bound to ask: is this just another scare, which will soon be forgotten about? After all, there have been many doomsday scenarios described in recent years. The increasing level of carbon dioxide in the atmosphere due to human activities, especially the cutting down and burning of the tropical rain forests, was going to launch us into a new ice age. Aerosols from spray cans were going to destroy the ozone layer high in the earth's atmosphere and subject us to intolerable doses of ultraviolet radiation from the sun. The population explosion and the exhaustion of oil reserves were going to bring about world-wide economic collapse. DDT and other pesticides and industrial chemicals were going to cause the extinction of many species on land, in the air and in the oceans.

In some ways the present epoch is a little like the late fifteenth century when the imminent approach of the year 1500 gave birth to many apocalyptic speculations, seen for example in Leonardo da Vinci's fascination in his sketches and writings with the subject of the Deluge. Perhaps the current doomsday atmosphere will lighten when the year 2000 is past. A good example of the genre is the *Doomsday Book* by Gordon Rattray Taylor, written in 1970, where some of the doomsday scenarios I mentioned above and several others are discussed.

Now it is true that none of these dire predictions has yet come to pass. In some cases, for example, the concern about aerosols from spray cans, the predicted effect was simply not as bad as had been feared. In the case of carbon dioxide, some climatologists now predict that the increased levels in the atmosphere due to our activities will have the rather welcome effect of preventing any further ice ages from occurring. But the reason that other doomsday scenarios have not been realized is that very determined action has been taken to prevent them. The dramatic population explosion in China, for example, has been taken under control by government edict and by mass education. Industrial chemicals are taken off the market if they are found to have dangerous side effects. The world oil crisis led to enormous efforts to reduce consumption through insulation and other measures.

The same must hold for the nuclear winter effect. There will be a period of a few years during which scientists will try to check the reality of the effect. If the nuclear winter prediction survives this scrutiny, then this is a scare that can only be made to go away by drastic action, especially the reduction and, in the end, elimination of the nuclear arsenals.

Chapter 2

The reality of the nuclear winter

The effects of a 1-megaton H-bomb explosion

In the event of a global nuclear war, the nuclear winter will be of little importance to many of the world's people, particularly those living in the cities or near military targets in the NATO or Warsaw pact countries. Even though much has been written about Hiroshima and Nagasaki, and many films and documentaries have tried to convey the horror of nuclear war, most people find it impossible to grasp the scale of destruction and suffering which nuclear war will bring. This can be the only explanation of the fact that the majority of the populations of countries like the United States, Britain, France and the Soviet Union acquiesce in their governments' continuing to base their defence strategy on nuclear weapons and on an ever-expanding nuclear arms race. Of course many people are strongly opposed to nuclear weapons and the deployment of Cruise and Pershing missiles has led to widespread opposition throughout Europe. Opinion polls in Britain show a majority against the deployment of Cruise missiles and the replacement of the Polaris submarine-launched missile with the much more expensive and powerful Trident missile. Yet in the 1983 General Election, opposition to nuclear

weapons was seen to be a serious electoral disad-
vantage for the Labour Party. Perhaps people are
persuaded by the argument that there has been peace
between the superpowers for 40 years and that nuclear
weapons have preserved this peace. The latest developments in missile technology make this argument
look very weak. The accuracy of today's weapons
means that an opponent's weapons can be destroyed in
their bunkers and make a 'first strike' attack look
increasingly attractive. The very short warning given
of a cruise missile attack means that retaliation has to
be decided upon and carried out within minutes of the
first warning, with horrific possibilities of accidental
nuclear war. Supporters of nuclear weapons do not
usually bother with such subtleties, though. It is
always easier to appeal to people's sense of patriotism,
to make them feel, in the case of countries like France
and Britain, that we are a more important and powerful
nation because of these weapons, and in the case of the
superpowers, that the other side is always just about to
achieve nuclear superiority.

When a 1-megaton hydrogen bomb explodes, the
blast, equivalent to the explosion of 1 million tons of
conventional explosive, is sufficient to completely
flatten all buildings within a radius of several miles.
The consensus of American and Japanese studies,
which appears to be disputed only by the British Home
Office in its foolish pamphlet *Domestic Nuclear Shelters: Technical Guidance*, is that almost everyone (98%)
within a 2-mile radius of the explosion would be killed
instantly by the blast. Ordinary houses would be
damaged beyond repair out to 5 miles and all windows
and doors would be blown in out to 10 miles.

The second consequence of the explosion is the development of an intense fireball, the temperature of which is initially about 20 million °C. The heat from this is so great that the clothes of people in the open or near windows catch fire and their exposed skin is charred in terrible burns. This can happen up to 5 miles from the explosion. The heat also starts widespread fires. In houses, curtains and furniture suddenly catch fire. Petrol stations, gas works, trees, plants – everything that can burn does so. Individual fires may join together to make one enormous conflagration which keeps on spreading outwards until there is nothing left to burn. There is also a strong possibility that a 'fire-storm' will develop, such as those experienced during the Second World War in Hamburg, Dresden and Hiroshima. Hurricane-force winds are sucked in by the fire and temperatures of 1000 °C or more can be reached, sufficient to melt glass and some metals. Any people trapped within the fire-storm would be incinerated or suffocated, even if they had managed to shelter from the blast.

Terrible though the effects of the blast and the fireball are, the greatest number of deaths is likely to be from radioactive fall-out. When a nuclear bomb explodes near the ground (these are called 'groundbursts' by the nuclear strategists) large quantities of soil and debris are swept up into the air. The intense radiation from the nuclear explosion makes this soil and dust radioactive. Along with the remains of the bomb itself, the material is sucked up into the air to form the familiar mushroom cloud high in the earth's atmosphere. The larger particles and debris fall to the ground in a matter of hours or days, spreading lethal doses of radiation over hundreds of square miles. Only those protected in deep concrete bunkers will be safe from the effects of fall-out. Naturally only very important people, for example those who have been responsible for our nuclear strategy, will have places in such bunkers.

Scientists have estimated, in a detailed caculation of the effects of an attack with five hydrogen bombs on the Greater London area, that out of a population of 7 million, over 5 million would be killed and a further half million injured, leaving only just over a million uninjured. 4 million of the deaths would be from the effects of radiation – a slow, lingering and awful death which may take up to 6 weeks. A widespread misapprehension about the effects of a nuclear war is that most people will die instantly. Unfortunately this is far from the reality.

It has been estimated that in the United States, out of a population of 230 million people, between 125 and 170 million people would die in a large scale nuclear war, with an additional 30 to 50 million people experiencing injuries requiring medical attention, all from the immediate and direct effects of the nuclear explosions themselves. A World Health Organization study has predicted that there would be over 1 billion fatalities and a further 1 billion additional injuries world-wide from blast and other immediate effects of an all-out nuclear war.

But let us not dwell on the fate of those within 20 miles or so of an H-bomb explosion. The nuclear strategists have estimated that even if all cities and large towns in the United States were destroyed by nuclear weapons, a third of the population would survive the attack. Let us turn our attention now to the fate of these survivors.

The aftermath of nuclear war – the official view

The British Home Office's pamphlet *Protect and Survive* gives an idea of how we are supposed to survive a nuclear war. Because 'No part of the United Kingdom can be considered safe from both the direct effects of the weapons and the resultant fall-out', the evacuation of urban areas is discouraged. The roads must be kept clear for missile launchers to scurry around and the Government has no desire to cope with hordes of refugees fleeing from urban areas and target zones. We are supposed to stay put in our homes and if we do not we are threatened with having our homes taken over by the Local Authority and with not being fed in the area we flee to.

We are then supposed to construct an emergency shelter inside our home, assuming that we have not been wise enough to build a proper concrete one in our garden (or be important enough to have a place in a Government bunker). A basement would be the best place assuming that you are one of the three and half per cent of London's population, for example, who have access to one. Alternatively a table covered with as much heavy material as possible in a ground-floor room. This sounds about as effective as the drill which all children in American primary schools learn for emergencies like earthquakes or nuclear attack – hide under the nearest table. Those who live in bungalows or caravans should 'arrange to shelter with someone close by': alternatively 'your Local Authority will be able to advise you what do do'. Those who live in the top two floors of blocks of flats should 'see their landlords now about alternative shelter accommodation'.

We then get in our shelter and wait there till we are told to come out. We are told that we should have 14 days supply of food and water with us. This may be difficult to get together within the few minutes of warning likely to be available to us of the impending attack. Unfortunately for much of the country it may not be 'safe', even within the Government's definition of what a safe dose of radiation is in wartime, to come out until a month after the nuclear exchange. Our radios and television will have been put out of action by a phenomenon known as the 'electro-magnetic pulse' — an intense burst of radio waves that accompanies a nuclear explosion — so we will have no idea what is going on or when it is 'safe'.

A Home Office internal circular points out that 'It can be said with absolute assurance that any widespread nuclear attack would quickly disrupt the distribution system for domestic and industrial water and much of the sewerage system.' It seems that thirst may be the major problem facing survivors in urban and many rural areas. Thirst will drive survivors from their shelters long before radiation levels have fallen to 'safe' levels. The breakdown of the sewage system will pose severe health hazards, with the re-emergence of diseases like typhus and cholera long since banished from our homes.

To look after us in these miserable days, the Government have devised an elaborate structure of national and regional seats of government, each with their own very safe and very well-equipped bunkers. Quite apart from the dangers posed by radiation, it may not be advisable for these national and regional governors to emerge from their bunkers and face the irate citizenry. Presumably actual control will rest in the hands of the military and their bunkers will be the very safest of all. From these the soldiery will be despatched through the irradiated landscape to tell us where to collect our food and water supplies and, most importantly, to round up 'potentially subversive people'.

In no time at all the farmers will be out harvesting the radioactive corn and planting the next crops. Since fuel will be in short supply, those with the foresight to keep a few horses will be in the strongest position. Careful Government calculations have shown that the dose we will receive from eating radioactive food is no greater than what we will have already received from fall-out, and is only a mere one hundred times the dose permitted in a year to workers in the nuclear power industry.

What numbers of survivors are we talking about? Back in 1960 Herman Kahn in his book *On Thermonuclear War* pointed out that even if the 50 largest cities and towns in the United States were totally destroyed, only one-third of the US population would have been killed. This is perhaps a representative figure for the casualties of the superpowers, figures that their nuclear strategists seem to believe represent acceptable losses. However several estimates for US casualties lie in the range 50–75 per cent of their population. For a European country like Britain with its much smaller land area and its widely dispersed

targets of cities, military bases, ports, radar install-
ations etc, it seems hard to believe that more than 10 or
20 per cent of the population would survive an all-out
attack.

The reality of the nuclear winter

What then does the nuclear winter effect mean for
those who have survived the direct effects of a nuclear
attack? Above the site of each nuclear explosion a huge
column of dust and smoke will rise, reaching up 5 or
10 miles or more into the atmosphere. These clouds
will spread out horizontally, rather like the 'anvil' of a
cumulonimbus storm cloud and then merge together.
The morning after the nuclear attack there will be
no dawn and the sky will be black at midday. This
blackness will last several weeks and during this time
the temperature will plummet downwards day by day.
For a location in the continental interior the temperature may drop by 40 °C (72 °F) in all, enough to turn
summer into winter and winter into arctic winer. For a
coastal site, much of Britan for example, the temperature drop will be much less, say 15 °C (27 °F), because
of the warming effect of the ocean. But this is still
enough to turn summer to winter, since our normal
climate is anyway much less dramatic than a continental climate, for exactly the same reason.

When we read of the dire consequences of the lost
summer of 1816, following the Tambora eruption, it is
not hard to imagine the much more severe consequences predicted for the nuclear winter. In the spring
or summer, the loss of sunlight and the severe cold
would destroy most crops, plants and trees. Rivers and

streams would freeze over and many animals would die of thirst, hunger or the cold. In the tropics, the effects would be catastrophic for plants and animals alike, whatever season the nuclear winter struck. Sunlight levels and temperatures are not expected to return to normal for at least three months. It is hardly surprising that the biologists see the nuclear winter as a possible major extinction event.

For human beings the consequences will be especially severe. The loss of the entire northern hemisphere harvest seems inevitable unless the nuclear war takes place in winter and the subsequent climatic effects are of short duration. This will mean starvation not only for many of the inhabitants of the northern hemisphere, but also for many southern hemisphere countries which are dependent on grain imports. It seems hard to imagine that many people in the northern hemisphere, even if they have survived the direct effects of the nuclear war, will be able to cope with the cold, hunger, dislocation of power, water, sewage and transport services, spread of epidemics, absence of medical aid, and the psychological stresses of the post-war period.

The main targets in a nuclear war are in the northern hemisphere and the black, radioactive cloud would be expected to spread over the whole hemisphere in a matter of weeks, bringing the suffering home to combatant and neutral nation alike. It is expected that the normal global weather patterns would be modified and that the cloud would soon spread into the southern hemisphere. Indeed it is hard to imagine that there are no targets in the southern hemisphere. Would the uranium mines and naval bases of South

Africa not be a target? Would not allies of the superpowers in the southern hemisphere be seen as a threat by their opponents? Whether or not nuclear weapons are detonated in the southern hemisphere, it is quite likely that they will suffer many of the dire consequences of the nuclear winter.

Chapter 3

What causes the nuclear winter?

The dust and smoke

To cause the greatest possible devastation at the site of a nuclear explosion, for example in an attack on a specific military target like a missile silo or radar installation, the bomb needs to be detonated near the ground. The nuclear strategists have coined the innocent sounding term 'groundburst', which makes it sound like a cloudburst or a balloon popping, for this type of explosion. The Hiroshima and Nagasaki atom bomb explosions, on the other hand, were detonated well above the ground. This type of explosion is called an 'airburst' and causes a more widespread, less concentrated blast.

In a groundburst, the explosion digs an enormous crater in the ground and throws huge quantities of earth and debris up into the air. Near 'ground zero' – the point of the explosion – rock would be vaporized by the force of the explosion. Further out, rock would be melted. Finally, at greater distances the rock would be pulverized and ejected from the crater. All these processes, together with the vaporized remains of the bomb and its casing, contribute to the dust carried up into the atmosphere by the fireball. The vaporized rock and metal and the liquid rock soon condense into small particles of dust. The intense radioactivity of the nuclear explosion makes all this debris radioactive. How long this radioactivity will last depends on the material. The bomb may be clad in a highly radioactive material like plutonium in order to increase the intensity of radioactivity in the debris. Such a bomb is called a 'dirty' bomb. However the ultimate 'clean' bomb is the 'neutron' bomb in which almost all the energy of the explosion goes into very energetic neutrons rather than into the blast. The neutrons are just as deadly as radioactivity and make everything they collide with radioactive. The purpose of the neutron bomb is to kill people but to leave buildings intact and seems to be based on the premise that the ideal type of victory in a war is one in which the enemy's population is eliminated but you can still (when the radioactivity permits) occupy their cities.

The larger pieces of debris from a groundburst fall back to earth immediately but a huge column of small particles of radioactive dust is thrown high into the earth's atmosphere. A nuclear explosion is accompanied by an immense convective updraught of air which helps to lift the dust up to the height of the temperature inversion in the earth's atmosphere known as the tropopause. Below the tropopause, in what is called the troposphere, the temperature of the air decreases with altitude and the atmosphere is liable to become convectively unstable. The troposphere is where most weather phenomena – clouds, storms, fronts, etc – take place. Above the tropopause, in what is known as the stratosphere, the temperature of the air increases with altitude and the atmosphere is much more stable. The height of the tropopause above the ground varies from about 6 miles at the poles to about 11 miles at the equator, but it also depends on the climatic conditions. When the column of dust reaches the tropopause it starts to spread out horizontally to give the familiar mushroom-shaped cloud which we all hope never to see with our own eyes. This is rather like a speeded-up version of the development of a cumulonimbus storm cloud at a cold front: this too spreads out to form an 'anvil' when it reaches the tropopause. In more powerful nuclear explosions, with yields of 1 megaton or more, the dust will be driven far up into the stratosphere, to altitudes ranging from 15 miles for a 1-megaton bomb to 30 miles for a 50-megaton bomb.

The dust generated in groundbursts is the first ingredient of the nuclear winter effect. The second is the smoke created in the widespread fires that accompany a nuclear explosion. The fireball which forms when a H-bomb explodes is so intense that for miles around everything that can burn will burn. In rural areas, grass, trees, crops, plants, will ignite and start wildfires which may take weeks to burn out. In urban areas houses, factories, petrol stations, chemical plants will be consumed in conflagrations the like of which have not been seen before. The smoke plumes from these fires will reach to a height of many miles. Where fire-storm conditions are created, the smoke is likely to be driven up into the stratosphere.

Naturally it is not an easy matter to estimate how much dust and smoke are likely to be generated in an all-out nuclear war. However there are a few lines of evidence to help us. Firstly there is the experience of the H-bomb tests which took place in the atmosphere prior to the Nuclear Test Ban Treaty of 1963. These showed that between 1 and 6 tons of dust are thrown up into the mushroom cloud per megaton of explosive yield in a groundburst. They also showed that the typical size of the dust particles was a few tenths of a micron (1 micron is one thousandth of a millimetre).

For the fires caused by the nuclear war we have to base our predictions on urban conflagrations triggered by natural disasters like earthquakes, on wartime city fires started by incendiary bombs, on the experience of Hiroshima and Nagasaki, on massive wildfires and forest fires, and on experimental large-scale fires started to study the development of fires and smoke plumes.

Earthquakes have started urban conflagrations by breaking gas mains, disrupting fuel storage tanks, shorting electrical circuits and breaching open fires. Effective firefighting tends to be seriously hampered in a large earthquake. Spectacular large fires followed the 1906 San Francisco earthquake and that in Tokyo in 1923. A nuclear blast represents a much greater fire threat than a major earthquake, though.

The conventional bombing of Hamburg on 27–28 July 1943 and of Dresden on 13–14 February 1945 during the Second World War showed how easily a mass fire can be started in a city. Fires burned over many square miles and firestorm conditions were created. Within the fire zones almost all buildings were gutted and all combustible materials burned. Thick, dark smoke plumes rose to altitudes of 4 to 8 miles. A firestorm was created at Hiroshima, too, though at Nagasaki the hilly terrain resulted in a less dramatic conflagration.

Large-scale experimental fires have been studied in France and the United States and these help to define the height to which a smoke plume is expected to rise and the conditions for the generation of a firestorm. Many catastrophic forest fires have been recorded during the past century and areas of up to 10,000 square miles have been burned. The Peshtigo fires of 1871, in which 3000 square miles were burned along both banks of the Green Bay, Wisconsin, created a smoke plume which obscured the sun for 200 miles around. The gloom persisted, even at noon, for a week. The smoke plume from the 1933 fire in Tillamook County, Oregon, one of the most intense in recorded American experience, reached an altitude of 8 miles. Over 10,000 square miles were consumed in the Alaskan fires of 1957. These catastrophic forest fires tend to occur when the wood is particularly dry and vulnerable. Forest fires started in a nuclear war would probably not spread so easily, though they might be ignited at many different points of the forest. A more representative historical event might be the great Tunguska meteorite, which fell over Siberia on 30 June 1908, with a blast energy equivalent to about 10 megatons. Roughly 800 square miles of Siberian forest was flattened and eyewitnesses described 'burning falling trees' and widespread fires, which burned for 5 days.

In their calculations of the amount of smoke generated in a nuclear war the TTAPS group estimated that for a nuclear bomb exploded over a city, the fire zone would extend over 100 square miles for each megaton of explosive yield, with a somewhat smaller figure, on average, for the wildfires in rural areas.

About 200 tons of smoke would be generated per square mile or urban fire zone and about one-third as much from the rural wildfires. Altogether in a large-scale nuclear war between the superpowers in which 5000 megatons are exploded, the TTAPS scientists estimate that 225 million tons of smoke and 65 million tons of dust would be injected into the earth's atmosphere. This is rather similar to the estimate of the amount of dust thrown into the atmosphere by the Tambora volcanic eruption, 200 million tons. However the smoke turns out to be much more effective at absorbing sunlight and cooling the earth and so the consequences are far worse in the nuclear winter.

How long do the dust and smoke stay up?

Smoke and dust are injected into the earth's atmosphere all the time, of course, by factories, fires, winds. It is estimated that about 200 million tons of smoke are injected into the earth's atmosphere every year. Normally the particles of smoke and dust do not rise to very great altitudes and they usually fall to the ground or are washed out by rain or snow within a few days. We have all noticed how clear the air looks after it has rained. However if, as in the case of nuclear war, the particles are driven up to the upper troposphere (5 to 10 miles up, say) it takes longer for them to reach the ground, several weeks or more. And if dust or smoke particles reach the stratosphere, at an altitude of 10 miles or more, then they may stay up there for a year or more. The reason for this is that rain clouds hardly ever form in the stratosphere so the main way for particles to reach the ground is to drift down under gravity, which they do very slowly if they are small.

Naturally-occurring wildfires tend to inject smoke particles into the atmosphere to a height of 3 or 4 miles. Large urban fires have been known to inject smoke to twice that altitude. Two effects are likely to drive the smoke from a nuclear war to a much higher altitude: firstly the unprecedented scale of the fires expected to be started by large nuclear explosions and secondly the convective updraughts associated with the fire-storms which would develop where several bombs are exploded within a relatively small area. The detailed calculations of the TTAPS scientists show that about 5 per cent of the smoke generated in a nuclear war would reach the stratosphere.

How high the dust from nuclear explosions rises depends on the size of the bomb. A 1-megaton explosion can excavate a crater hundreds of yards in diameter and eject several million tons of debris, of which 10 to 30 thousand tons of small dust particles will reach the stratosphere. A 'low-yield burst', as the nuclear strategists like to call a 100-kiloton explosion (only five times more powerful than the Hiroshima bomb), would probably not drive any dust into the stratosphere.

In addition to the height to which the dust and smoke are driven there are two other factors which affect how long the nuclear winter lasts. The first is that, particularly while the smoke is rising in a dense plume, the smoke particles will tend to coagulate together to form larger particles. This has the effect, firstly, that the particles will fall to the ground faster, and secondly that the particle radius may grow bigger than the critical 1-micron size below which the particles are most effective at absorbing and scattering sunlight. The second effect, which I have already mentioned above, is that dust and smoke particles tend to be collected up, or 'scavenged', by drops of water and then carried to the ground as rain. Both these effects, coagulation and wash-out by rain, are included in the TTAPS group calculation.

The net effect, according to the calculations of the TTAPS scientists, is that the sky would remain dark or gloomy for a time between one and six months, depending on the assumptions made about the number and yield of the warheads used, the properties of the dust and smoke particles, and the rate at which they are washed out.

The pall of dust and smoke spreads out

Picture the scene you might see from a space station circling the earth in the aftermath of a nuclear war. Everywhere that bombs have been exploded a column of dust and black smoke is rising from the ground and then spreading out. Gradually these plumes merge into one huge band of dust circling the northern latitudes of the earth. At first this band would be very patchy, the darkest areas lying over the devastated countries of the combatants. But after a few days the band rings the whole earth and starts to spread northwards towards the pole and southwards towards the equator. In a matter of weeks the southern hemisphere, too, is covered by the dark cloud. No part of the globe is safe from the effects of a nuclear winter.

How dark would it be on earth at this stage? In their 'baseline' case, which is what they regard as their best bet, the TTAPS scientists estimate that only 3 per cent of the solar radiation normally incident on the earth would reach the ground. This would be gloomier than a dark, overcast winter's day. The dimming effect is almost entirely caused by the smoke particles in the atmosphere, since these are highly effective at absorbing visible radiation. The dust particles, on the other hand, tend mainly to scatter or reflect sunlight and so much of this radiation still reaches the ground. This is similar to the normal effect of a cloud passing in front of the sun. Even though the sun's disc may no longer be visible, showing that the direct transmission of sunlight has fallen to a a very low value, the day does not suddenly become pitch black. The small droplets of water in the cloud scatter the sunlight and much of it still reaches the ground.

While the pall of dust and smoke from a nuclear war is still spreading out and merging into a single shroud, there will be large areas of the earth covered with much darker clouds than average. In these areas the amount of sunlight reaching the ground may drop to one millionth of normal, which is about the level of a moonlit night. This would put an end to photosynthesis, the process by which plants absorb energy from sunlight in order to grow. If this daytime darkness persisted for weeks or months, there would be a climatic catastrophe far worse than the baseline case I am describing.

How cold will it get?

Working out how cold the earth gets in a nuclear winter turns out to be one of the most complex parts of the whole calculation and is critical to the whole argument of the severity of the phenomenon. As it happens, for the past ten years or so I have been studying the way that clouds of dust and soot absorb starlight. When a star like the sun begins to die it grows enormously in size to become a red giant star and starts to throw off its outer layers in a strong wind. Once the gas in this wind has travelled sufficiently far from the star, elements like silicon, magnesium, aluminium, iron, and oxygen combine together and condense out to form small, solid particles of aluminium and magnesium silicates, similar in composition to the earth's rocks. The star therefore finds itself surrounded by a cloud of silicate dust which absorbs the star's light. If the star has an unusually high abundance of the element carbon, the chemistry proceeds a bit differently. The oxygen combines with carbon to form carbon monoxide and the excess carbon condenses out as small sooty particles.

Astronomers have developed a considerable expertise in understanding the effect these clouds of silicate dust or soot have on starlight and this expertise can be applied to the nuclear winter calculations. Of course the geometry of the situation is rather different. In the nuclear winter calculation the dust and smoke cloud surrounds the earth, not the sun. But the success we have had in understanding the flow of stellar radiation through dust gives us some confidence in the nuclear winter calculations.

To see that the calculation of the temperature of the surface of the earth after a nuclear holocaust is not a simple matter, let us try to estimate the earth's temperature in a naive way. The law of conservation of energy tells us that when the earth receives the sun's energy, it has to radiate this energy away again. How much energy a body like the earth radiates depends on its temperature. To a good approximation the amount of energy radiated depends on the fourth power of the temperature above absolute zero. (This is called Stefan's law, after the Austrian physicist Josef Stefan.) Now absolute zero is about -273 °C, so if we take the average temperature of the earth as 13 °C, the earth is 286 degrees above absolute zero. Now suppose that the amount of radiation impinging on the earth is reduced by a factor of 30, as in the TTAPS scientists' baseline case. The fourth root of 30 is about 2.2, so the earth's temperature should go down to 129 degrees above absolute zero, or -144 °C! This would mean an instant end to life on earth. However, something very important has been neglected in the above sum and that is the heat energy radiated at infrared wavelengths by the dust cloud. The law of conservation of energy applies to the particles of dust and smoke too and they have to radiate away the energy they absorb from the sun's light. They do this at infrared wavelengths and the earth is therefore bathed in infrared radiation, which to some extent compensates for the visible radiation of which the cloud has deprived us.

Another simple calculation shows that there is a second complication. I mentioned above that the average temperature of the earth, averaged over its surface and over the year, is about 13 °C. We can use Stefan's law to find out what temperature we would have expected the earth to have in order for the heat it radiates to balance the energy it receives from sunlight. The answer comes out to be -23 °C (250 degrees above absolute zero). In some mysterious way the earth is radiating away 70 per cent more energy than it receives!

This paradox turns out to be a consequence of the earth having an atmosphere. The molecules of the air, especially the carbon dioxide and water, are strong absorbers of infrared radiation, though they are almost transparent to visible light. When the earth radiates away its infrared radiation, this cannot all escape. A good chunk of this infrared radiation is absorbed by the molecules of the atmosphere, which then radiate the energy away again, also at infrared wavelengths. But the molecules radiate in all directions and so about half of their energy comes back down to the earth again. Thus the reason the earth is so much warmer than expected is that it is being heated up by the earth's atmosphere, as well as by the direct sunlight. This phenomenon is known as the 'greenhouse' effect, by analogy with the principle of an ordinary greenhouse. In the latter it is the glass walls and roof of the greenhouse which play the role of the molecules in the earth's atmosphere in absorbing infrared radiation from the plants and other objects inside the greenhouse.

In practice if the dust and smoke particles at any particular altitude absorb sunlight and get heated up, then they will heat up the air molecules around them and share their heat energy with the molecules. Since the air molecules are more efficient radiators of infrared radiation than the dust and smoke particles, the main warming of the earth tends to be because of the heating of the atmosphere and the resulting increased 'greenhouse' warming, rather than due to direct warming by the dust and smoke cloud.

So the average temperature of the earth in a nuclear winter depends on these competing effects: the loss of direct heating by sunlight due to absorption or to reflection back into space by dust or smoke; the heating from the cloud of dust and smoke; and the heating from the earth's atmosphere. Now it makes quite a big difference whether the dust and smoke are at high altitudes, in the stratosphere say, or are much lower down. Seventy-five per cent of the mass of the earth's atmosphere is in the lower 6 miles. A cloud of dust and smoke 1 mile up will lie below most of the atmosphere, whereas one 10 miles up will lie above most of it. If the cloud of dust and smoke does lie above most of the atmosphere, then the infrared radiation which it (and the air molecules it has heated up) directs downwards towards the earth will be heavily absorbed by the atmosphere. As a result the temperature on the ground will be much colder than if the same cloud of dust and smoke were at low altitudes. Appendix A (p.103) gives a very simple version of the calculation of the ground temperature corresponding to these two extremes, for different amounts of dimming by dust and smoke, and for an intermediate case which is more representative of the nuclear winter situation, where the dust and smoke is assumed to be spread throughout the main part of the atmosphere. This shows that even if the cloud of dust and smoke cut out all the direct sunlight, the average temperature would only drop about 24 °C (43 °F) for a low-altitude cloud, whereas for a high altitude cloud the temperature drop would be about 75 °C. For the intermediate, more realistic case, the maximum temperature drop, corresponding to all the sunlight being absorbed, would be 46 °C (83 °F). The nuclear winter calculations predict that the direct sunlight would be dimmed, on average, to anything between 35 per cent and 0.0001 per cent of its normal value, depending on the number of bombs exploded, the types of target, and the amount of smoke and dust generated. The simple calculation of the Appendix shows that even for the optimistic case of 35 per cent of the sun's visible light being transmitted, the average ground temperature would drop by 39 °C (70 °F) for a high-altitude cloud, though only by 14 °C (25 °F) for a low-altitude cloud. For the intermediate case, the simple calculation of Appendix A predicts a temperature drop of 26 °C (47 °F). The detailed calculation by the TTAPS scientists takes into account many factors neglected in the simple calculation given in Appendix A. Firstly we have to consider to what extent the different types of particle which are present absorb light or scatter (i.e. reflect) it. Secondly their models take account of the actual distribution of dust through the atmosphere. They find that in their baseline case, the average ground temperature in a continental interior will drop by about 35 °C (63 °F) within the first fortnight after a nuclear war, and will not rise above freezing for three months or so. As we shall see this could have a catastrophic effect on many of the world's plant and animal species. And in other more extreme but equally plausible scenarios, the temperature is predicted to have dropped by more than 50 °C (90 °F), to below − 40 °C (− 40°F), after a few weeks, and to remain below − 40 °C for several months. In these more severe scenarios the temperature is not expected to rise above freezing point until a year after the holocaust.

The effect on the earth's climate

The temperature calculations described above take account only of the direct effects of the lost sunlight on the temperature of the ground and could be taken as representative of the effects on a continental interior at mid-latitudes. The actual weather we experience from day to day and the climate of any particular region of the earth depend in a complex way on the circulation of the atmosphere and the oceans. The oceans cover some 70 per cent of the earth's surface, to an average depth of over 2 miles. The enormous heat capacity of the oceans can be illustrated by the fact that even if the sun were switched off for one year, the average temperature of the oceans would go down by only about 1 °C (2 °F). The oceans therefore act to even out any changes in temperature that occur on land as a result of reduction in solar heating. They do this through large-scale circulations in the oceans, which transfer warm water from the tropics towards northern and southern latitudes. In Britain we are the direct beneficiaries of one of these large-scale circulations, in the form of the Gulf Stream. The combined effects of the Gulf Stream and the prevailing westerly winds make Britain on average 9 °C (16 °F) warmer than the average for its latitude. The differences in temperature between land and ocean and between the tropics and the poles also drive large scale circulations in the earth's atmosphere, the winds. These too tend to equalize extremes of temperature. For example the average amount of solar energy reaching the ground at the equator is twice the average for a general location on the earth. If this was reflected in the actual ground temperature, then the average temperature on the equator would be 67 °C (153 °F), instead of the 25–30 °C (77–86 °F) actually measured. This is because a large-scale convective instability of the lower atmosphere (the troposphere) drives hot air vertically upwards and draws in cooler air from higher latitudes. This large-scale circulation of the atmosphere at the tropics is known as a Hadley cell.

Each evening as the sun sets, the ground starts to cool down. In a continental interior where the temperature is mainly determined by the direct solar heating of the ground, the contrast in temperature between day and night is 10 to 15 °C (18 to 27 °F). At a coastal site on the other hand, for example over much of Britain, the average temperature contrast is only 4 or 5 °C (9 °F) between day and night. A similar contrast between continental and maritime sites is seen in the variation of temperature through the seasons. In the continental interior of the United States, for example, the average temperature in midwinter is about 35 °C (63 °F) colder than the average temperature in midsummer, while in Britain the average midwinter temperature is only about 10 °C (18 °F) colder than the midsummer temperature.

How would the nuclear winter modify the climate? This is a very complex question which can not yet be fully answered. Scientists have succeeded in making highly simplified computer simulations of the global climate which reproduce the main features of the world's average weather. Groups of scientists in both the USA and USSR have tested the effect of introducing a cloud of dust and smoke covering northern latitudes into these computer models. These calculations confirm that the climate would be drastically modified. The American study, by Curt Covey, Stephen Schneider and Starley Thompson of the National Center for Atmospheric Research (NCAR), Boulder, Colorado, consider a case somewhat less severe than the TTAPS baseline case and follow its evolution for some three weeks after the hypothetical nuclear war. They find that the average land cooling 10 days after a summer nuclear war would be 15–20 °C (27–36 °F) and that much of the northern hemisphere, particularly North America and the Soviet Union would reach temperatures well below freezing. The Soviet study, by Vladimir Aleksandrov, head of the Climate Research Laboratory at the Computing Centre of the USSR Academy of Sciences, Moscow, and colleagues, takes a case rather more extreme than the TTAPS baseline case and follows its evolution for more than a year. The average temperature drop after 40 days ranges from 15 °C (27 °F) at latitude 30 degrees north to over 20 °C (36 °F) at latitude 60 degrees north. Large areas of the Northern hemisphere would experience temperature drops of 30–40 °C (54–72 °F) during the first month after a nuclear war. Even after 8 months the average temperature of the northern hemisphere is still 10 °C (18 °F) cooler than normal. An important prediction of the models is that the changes to the atmospheric temperature profile essentially brings the tropopause down to much lower altitudes, almost to the ground in fact. The stable conditions of the stratosphere, where rain clouds rarely form, therefore extend to much lower altitudes than normal. Dust and smoke particles will therefore not be washed out of the atmosphere as fast as the TTAPS scientists have assumed, and this may prolong the nuclear winter still further.

Unfortunately these simulations of the effects of a cloud of dust and smoke on climate are not yet able to test the effect of the atmospheric circulation on the cloud. In particular they cannot answer the key question whether the dust and smoke cloud would cross the equator (assuming there have been no targets in the southern hemisphere) and cover the whole globe. However there are already clear signs that the normal pattern of atmospheric circulation in the tropics would be disrupted. The normal spring or summer pattern is of hot air rising at the equator and dividing into two air streams, one flowing northwards and the other southwards. These two streams make up the circulation pattern in the tropics, which we have met above, the Hadley cells. In the NCAR simulations of the spring war in the northern hemisphere, this pattern is disrupted and a single cell carrying air upwards in the northern hemisphere, across the equator and then down at southern latitudes, is created. This strongly suggests that the southern hemisphere would be shrouded in dust and smoke within a matter of weeks. At other seasons dust and smoke will be transported across the equator in a more irregular manner, but the outcome may well be the same. However this particular NCAR simulation included only atmospheric smoke in the calculation and Starley Thompson reports (*Climatic Change*, June 1984) that when stratospheric dust is added to the calculation the Hadley cell pattern is not disrupted.

Thus the fate of the southern hemisphere remains an open issue.

For Britain and Western Europe, the Soviet global circulation model indicates that the temperature drop would be 15–25 °C (27–45 °F) after 40 days, and only about 5 °C (9 °F) after 8 months (some areas, like Spain, might be back to normal temperatures). These figures show that spring or summer would be converted to a severe winter and that winter would be converted to arctic winter. Since much of Europe would be destroyed in all-out nuclear war and radioactivity levels would be intolerable over most of the area, the nuclear winter merely administers the final blow to the remaining small groups of survivors. Moreover the drastic changes to the global weather pattern means a coastal region like Britain will be buffeted by terrible storms which will worsen the effects of the temperature drop for the survivors.

Testing the nuclear winter predictions

Of course the full horror of the nuclear winter predictions can be tested in only one way, a way that the nuclear strategists and our political leaders seem only too ready to contemplate. However it is still possible to test the computer models being used in these calculations against other related types of phenomena, namely the Martian dust storms and volcanic eruptions on earth. In fact before the TTAPS group of scientists had ever thought about the climatic effects of nuclear war, they had been working on the problem of the Martian dust storms, which first came to their attention during the Mariner 9 project in 1971. As the spacecraft orbited Mars, the first to do so round another planet, they were able to measure the temperature both of the surface of the planet and of the thin Martian atmosphere. They found that the planet was cooler than normal during the dust storm, which covered the entire planet, and that the atmosphere was warmer than normal. This was entirely to be expected since the dust was absorbing the sun's radiation and thereby getting warmer itself as well as cooling the planet's surface. The computer models they constructed were able to reproduce their observations accurately. They then decided to turn their attention to terrestrial problems and started to consider the cooling effect of the dust ejected in volcanic eruptions. Again the models explained the small drop in the average temperature of the earth, typically about 0.5 to 1 °C, following major volcanic eruptions. The most detailed studies so far are of the Mexican volcano, El Chichon, which erupted in late March and early April 1982. Although not a particularly large eruption, El Chichon injected unusually large amounts of volcanic material into the stratosphere and scientists have been able to follow the evolution of the dust veil using satellites and ground-based laser ranging techniques. They have also been able to sample the dust and to monitor the temperature changes underneath the cloud, which spread around the globe within a few weeks of the eruption. This study is still continuing.

Of course the nuclear winter predictions are much more severe than either of these cases, but they do show that the models are capable of modelling accurately the consequences of dust and smoke injected into a planetary atmosphere. In the future we may expect to see even more elaborate computer models of the development of the nuclear winter and these will resolve some of the still unanswered questions. I will discuss some of the uncertainties of the nuclear winter calculations further in Chapter 5.

Chapter 4

Crisis for life on earth

The effect of the nuclear winter on crops and plants

A nuclear war would bring enormous destruction of crops and plants through devastating wildfires and radioactive fallout. A study carried out by the US Brookhaven National Laboratory on Long Island, New York, illustrates the effects of radioactivity on plants. A large source of radioactivity was placed in the middle of a carefully selected forest. Trees in general were the most vulnerable, especially the pine trees, and were eliminated in a large swathe, leaving an otherwise intact community of shrubs, grasses and herbs, mosses and lichens. At higher exposures the woody shrubs were killed; at higher levels still, the herbs and grasses; and finally at still higher exposures, only certain mosses and lichens survived. Within each group, the lower-growing, smaller-bodied forms were the most resistant. In general the species most vulnerable to any type of severe change in habitat are those with large bodies and long reproductive cycles. The most resistant are those with small bodies and high reproductive potential. The latter include the species that compete effectively with humans, the 'pests', weeds and insects of the garden, the species of the roadside and derelict site.

But from the effects of radioactivity and wildfires alone, most plant species would recover if not within months then within years. We can even imagine the stricken human survivors restarting some kind of agriculture. In countries not directly involved in the conflict, life might have gone on as usual.

The nuclear winter changes all that. The extended period of darkness or twilight following a nuclear war would put an end to the growth of plants, which depend on sunlight for growth through the process of photosynthesis. When the light level falls below about 5 per cent of normal, plants can no longer produce any net growth. After a prolonged period of darkness many plants would simply die. This would apply both to green plants on the land and to the tiny green plants in the oceans known as algae (or phytoplankton, to give them their scientific name).

The subfreezing temperatures which a nuclear war would suddenly inflict on the environment are likely to have an even more drastic effect. The resistance of plants to cold depends on the time of year and on what they are used to. In regions where severe winters are experienced like northern Canada and Siberia the dormant buds of plants may be able to endure temperatures as low as $-80\ °C\ (-112\ °F)$, well below even the most extreme nuclear winter predictions. But in their growing season, these same plants may be killed if the temperature falls below $-10\ °C\ (14\ °F)$ In temperate regions like Britain the dormant buds of plants can tolerate temperatures ranging from -8 to $-25\ °C\ (+18$ to $-13\ °F)$, but are likely to be killed immediately by sub-zero temperatures in the spring or summer. This greater capacity to endure cold in the winter depends on the plant being preconditioned to cold temperatures, as occurs naturally in autumn and winter months. The sudden onset of severe cold, at any time except midwinter, is likely to be fatal to many plants. In the tropics, plants continue to grow all the year round and their tolerance to cold is very limited. The range of minimum temperatures that tropical plants can tolerate is from about -5 °C to $+5$ °C (23–41 °F). It is interesting to note that two-thirds of all species of plants animals and microorganisms live within 25 degrees of the equator.

The world's main agricultural crops are all extremely vulnerable to cold. Exposure of rice to a temperature of only 13 °C (55 °F) at the critical time can inhibit grain formation. Corn and soybeans are quite sensitive to temperatures below 10 °C (50 °F), while wheat is killed by temperatures below -5 °C (23 °F) if they occur during the summer months. If we now look at the temperatures predicted in the nuclear winter calculations, we see that the loss of one year's harvest of virtually all crops seems almost inevitable, whatever time of year the war takes place. Plant production on earth would drop to a very low level. Moreover even if light and temperature levels are restored to normal after a year, biologists estimate that it may take a decade or more for plant cover on earth and ocean to return to normal levels, given the many other stresses (radioactivity, excess ultraviolet radiation from the sun due to damage to the ozone layer, chemical pollution, foraging by animals) that plants will be subjected to.

Soil organisms are not directly dependent on sunlight and photosynthesis and can often remain dormant for long periods, so they would be relatively unaffected by the darkness, but might be vulnerable to extreme cold. In many areas the loss of plant cover would leave the soil susceptible to severe erosion by wind and water.

The effect on land-based animals and freshwater species

In a nuclear winter animals face a variety of potentially lethal stresses. Many will have received fatal doses of radioactivity. Those that survive the direct effects of nuclear war will face the problem that most sources of fresh water will be frozen to a depth of several feet. The cessation of plant growth because of the low levels of sunlight penetrating to the ground will cause starvation for many herbivores. The sudden reduction in the populations of these animals will in turn spell disaster for the carnivores. Animals that hibernate to survive winter need a full summer's build-up of fat reserves to last through a normal winter and will have little chance of enduring a sudden and drastic nuclear winter descending on them in spring or summer. There is the clear possibility of widespread extinctions of animal species, particularly among those found only in the northern hemisphere. It wil be extremely difficult for farmers to keep their livestock alive unless they have been well prepared for the onset of the sudden winter and are self-sufficient in fuel and feed.

Scavengers that could withstand the extreme cold would flourish in the post-war period because of the billions of unburied human and animal bodies. We may face a world in which rats, cockroaches and flies are the most prominent surviving creatures.

Many freshwater organisms would be killed by the combination of loss of sunlight and thick ice cover. Widespread extinctions can be expected amongst fish and other freshwater species. In the tropics animals, birds and fish are particularly ill-equipped to survive cold temperatures, quite apart from the effects of the damage to the tropical rain-forests due to the prolonged darkness and cold.

The effects on life in the oceans

The plants and animals of the oceans ought to have the best chance of survival since they are buffered from the effects of the cold by the huge thermal inertia of the oceans. I mentioned in Chapter 3 that even the loss of a year's radiation from the sun would reduce the average temperature of the ocean by only 1 °C (2 °F). However, things are not quite as rosy as that because most of the really warm waters of the oceans, those above 10 °C (50 °F), say, are confined to the upper few thousand feet of the oceans and amount to less than 10 per cent of the total volume of the oceans. These warmer waters might experience a cooling by as much as 5–10 °C (9–18 °F) in an extreme nuclear winter scenario, where the dimming of the sun lasts for the best part of a year. This is just the magnitude of the cooling estimated to have taken place in the major extinctions of tropical marine species found in the fossil record (see Ch.1).

The effect of prolonged darkness on marine organisms has been investigated in laboratory studies. Food chains composed of phytoplankton (algae), zooplankton (microscopic animals which live by eating the algae) and fish (which prey on the zooplankton) are especially vulnerable. After just a few days of darkness, the phytoplankton die off or go into a dormant stage. Within roughly two months in a temperate zone in late spring or summer, and within three to six months in winter, fish and other aquatic animals start to show drastic population declines. For many species this process could be irreversible. In the tropics the effects of prolonged darkness are likely to be even worse because nutrient reserves are lower and energy requirements for tropical animals are greater. In the polar regions where species are adapted to long dark winters, the effects would be much less severe.

For human survivors of a nuclear winter trying to fish in coastal waters, there is the added difficulty of the fierce storms that might occur in these waters. The large fishing vessels on which modern society depends for fish supplies may well have been destroyed in strikes on their home ports or will have difficulty obtaining fuel. Toxic wastes and silt running off the land are an added hazard to marine life in coastal waters.

The consequences for human beings

To grasp the full impact of the nuclear winter on human beings we have to appreciate first that all life is bound together in an interdependent unity. Scientists have coined the term 'biosphere' to describe the earth, atmosphere and oceans, and the life forms within them. Biologists have found that to understand an individual organism it is necessary to study the whole community of plants, animals, microbes, in which that organism lives, as well as the physical properties of its environment — the solar radiation, the gases which make up the air, the chemicals in the soil and in the water of streams and oceans. This study is called ecology and in recent years we have become much more sensitive about the ecological impact of human activities. The reason is not just that we care about the earth and its life. We depend on numerous ecosystems for our survival. We are dependent on plants and animals for food and we have to control their predators and diseases. It would be quite impossible for the present population of the world to survive as hunter-gatherers, as human beings did in prehistoric times. We are dependent on agriculture, on managed ecosystems. The most obvious and the most serious impact on human society of a nuclear winter is the probable destruction of one year's harvest of almost all crops and the very great difficulty there will be in re-establishing large-scale agriculture.

There is no danger, of course, of these agricultural crops becoming extinct in a nuclear winter. Seeds will be preserved in many locations over the earth and even the desperate and starved survivors of a nuclear war will understand that some of these must be saved for future planting. The problem will be that the selective extermination of insects, birds and animals will result in new pests flourishing; it is hard to believe that the distribution of fuel, fertilizers and pesticides, on which modern agriculture is utterly dependent, will return to normal for many years. The destruction of plant cover will result in soil erosion from bare, exposed land. Biologists estimate that the time-scale for recovery of agriculture is likely to be a decade. There would obviously be a very serious problem of sharing and distributing the surviving foodstocks. The loss of one year's harvest would be catastrophic for those many nations which are far from self-sufficient in their food production and are completely dependent on food imports.

The harvesting of food from the oceans is likely to be equally drastically curtailed by the nuclear winter and we have already seen that many food chains that provide essential nutrition for human beings are likely to be destroyed. In the more severe scenarios where the darkness is so severe that photosynthesis in the ocean ceases for many months, very many species of fish may be exterminated. There is therefore no guarantee that human beings can look to the oceans for salvation in the event of the loss of most land harvests.

Besides providing us with food, biological ecosystems perform many other essential services, on which we are almost equally dependent. They are responsible for the generation and preservation of soils, the recycling of nutrients, the controlling of potential agricultural pests and carriers of human disease, the disposal of waste products and dead organisms, the purification of fresh water supplies by microbial activity, and even the regulation of the climate (it is well known that aforestation of a region may be the first step towards the creation of a desert). Above all nature provides a vast genetic pool from which new varieties and species of plants and animal can evolve naturally or, crucially, by selective breeding.

Not all these services are, of course, threatened by the nuclear winter. But one of the problems is that the full biological consequences of a climatic catastrophe like the nuclear winter are very hard to predict. This detailed interdependence of the members of an ecological community make it both resistant to small changes and vulnerable to large changes.

If we concentrate solely on the direct consequences for human beings, then even if the darkness and cold spread over the entire planet, it seems unlikely that this would result in the immediate deaths of all the people of the southern hemisphere. On islands far from the sites of nuclear explosions and relatively free from radioactive fall-out, and where the temperature drop was moderated by the warming of the ocean, then there would be survivors. There would probably be survivors scattered throughout the southern hemisphere and, perhaps, even in some places in the northern hemisphere. But would these small groups of people be able to survive? They would be forced back into a hunter-gatherer existence, but without the knowledge of the environment that our hunter-gatherer ancestors accumulated over the millennia. They would be facing a new and malign enviroment, with high radiation levels, a severely damaged natural world, and unprecedented weather conditions. Social, economic and cultural systems would be shattered and human beings would face immense psychological stresses. It was the consensus of the group of distinguished biologists who met in Washington in October 1983 that:

> We could not exclude the possibility that the scattered survivors simply would not be able to rebuild their populations, that they would, over a

period of decades or even centuries, fade away. In other words, we could not exclude the possibility of a full-scale nuclear war entraining the extinction of homo sapiens.

These sombre words should be enought to halt us in our plunge towards destruction. What more needs to be said? How can we allow these stockpiles of weapons to continue to exist a moment longer? Life on earth will certainly go on after a nuclear holocaust, but it may go on without us. And all of human culture and civilization, the achievements of the past few thousands of years, will have been futile.

Chapter 5

How certain are the nuclear winter calculations?

The sceptics

Not everyone in the scientific community is convinced that the nuclear winter prediction is correct. The most prominent criticisms have come from Edward Teller in the United States and from John Maddox in Britain. Edward Teller is Associate Director of the Lawrence Livermore National Laboratory in California and is widely known as the father of the hydrogen bomb. Even before the first atom bomb had been made, he was already arguing that a much more powerful bomb could be made by recreating the conditions in the centre of the sun, where hydrogen is fused into helium. He was disappointed for some years that his proposal was not taken up, but when in August 1949 the Soviet Union succeeded in exploding an atom bomb, the go-ahead was given for the construction of what was then known as the 'super', under Teller's direction. Three years later the first H-bomb was exploded in the South Pacific. Teller has always been an ardent supporter of nuclear weapons, arguing that they have preserved the peace, through deterrence, for the past 40 years.

Writing in the British scientific magazine *Nature* 23 Aug 1984 Teller has attacked the TTAPS nuclear winter calculations as an exaggeration, claiming that if different assumptions are made about the nature and quantity of dust and smoke, then the effect becomes so small as to be unimportant. He has summed up his position in the words 'the concept of a severe climatic change must be considered dubious'. It is interesting that in the same article he argues that the effects of radioactive fall-out on non-combatant nations are not a matter of concern even though the average predicted dose is 20 rads, with hotspots of 250 rads (hundreds of times higher than the natural radiation background).

John Maddox is editor of *Nature* and a regular broadcaster on BBC radio. Because *Nature* is a prestigious magazine, which has published many profound and important papers, his two editorials on the subject of the nuclear winter (1 Mar. and 13 Dec. 1984) have attracted some attention. In the first he described the TTAPS calculations as less than convincing for two reasons: firstly that the detailed discussion of the assumptions had not been published, secondly that the 'pardonable simplicity of the calculation of climatic effects, innocent as it is of the feedback mechanisms likely to occur in the real atmosphere, is likely to exaggerate the severity of what is called the nuclear winter'. The first criticism is curious because the TTAPS paper, published in the American magazine *Science* in December 1983, contains eighty-seven detailed footnotes giving technical details and bibliographical references. The latter include the previous papers by some of the TTAPS authors on the Martian dust storms and on the effects of dust from terrestrial volcanoes, which give plenty of detail on the development of the TTAPS atmospheric models. The second criticism has some validity in that, as we saw in

Chapter 3, the actual temperature on the ground does not depend just on the flow of sunlight through the atmosphere and the nuclear smoke and dust cloud. Oceans and winds play an important role in reducing extremes of temperature between land and ocean and between equator and poles. However, the TTAPS authors make perfectly clear in their papers the limitations of their calculation and state clearly both that the temperature drop over the oceans would be very small and that land temperatures will not fall as sharply as their simple model predicts. They stated that 'Actual temperature decreases in continental interiors might be roughly 30 per cent smaller than predicted here, and along coastlines 70 per cent smaller.' These estimates are in line with the results of the Soviet and American global circulation models which do take into account some of these important meteorological effects. There is no serious calculation of the climatological consequences of a nuclear war which concludes that there is no nuclear winter effect. It is therefore hard to understand John Maddox's complacent conclusion that 'If, on the basis of calculations so far published, some people should refuse to believe that there would be a long winter after a nuclear war, they cannot easily be refuted.'

Maddox's second editorial was on the occasion of the publication of the report by the US National Research Council on 'The Effects on the Atmosphere of a Major Nuclear Exchange'. Perhaps to John Maddox's surprise, this weighty investigation had endorsed the nuclear winter effect as a real possibility. They conclude that:

In sum then, the various model results in concert with a limited set of observations of related natural phenomena provide a basis for concluding that a nuclear war scenario like the NRC baseline case could produce large temperature decreases near the surface ... for a period of weeks to months following the event ... Moreover, rapid spreading of particulates into the tropics and even into the southern hemisphere is a real possibility.

By concentrating on the range of uncertainties discussed in the report, John Maddox gives the impression that his earlier scepticism has been confirmed.

Edward Teller and John Maddox are not the only nuclear winter sceptics. Although presentation of the TTAPS results at the 1983 Washington conference appeared to result in a strong consensus among the American and Soviet scientists who took part in the debate, the result of a presentation by Richard Turco, Paul Ehrlich and Yuri Golytsin to a group of British scientists in Oxford in November 1984 had a different result. The contributions of many of the British scientists appeared to be rather negative, though none of the critics appeared to have performed any detailed calculations themselves. Although the overall response to the nuclear winter effect among British scientists has displayed less concern than their American and Soviet colleagues, some excellent work is being done, particularly under the auspices of the group Scientists Against Nuclear Arms (SANA). Valuable accounts of the nuclear winter have been written by Christopher Meredith, Owen Greene and Mike Pentz of the Open University; by my colleague

Ian Percival of Queen Mary College, London; and others (see Suggestions for Further Reading, p.113).

In this chapter I will discuss some of the uncertainties in the nuclear winter calculations, drawing heavily on the report of the US National Research Council mentioned above. The US National Research Council Consists of the US National Academy of Sciences and the US National Academy of Engineering and was commissioned to investigate the climatic consequences of a nuclear war by the US Department of Defense. The investigation was carried out by a committee of 18 eminent scientists, chaired by George Carrier of Harvard University, and after carefully defining what they considered to be the most likely nuclear war scenario, they persuaded atmospheric physicists and climatologists to run their computer programmes to test the consequences of it. Their report runs to some 200 closely-argued pages.

The nuclear war scenario

Whether or not a nuclear war is followed by drastic climatic change depends strongly, obviously, on the scale and type of war. Current NATO strategies involve responding to a Soviet tank invasion of West Germany with tactical nuclear weapons. However, even though the official line is that a nuclear war could be contained at any particular level of escalation, few strategists really believe that is what would happen. In a time of tension, events are likely to move very fast. Once either side have made a decision to use nuclear weapons, it is very tempting to go for an all-out first strike against the other side's weapons, to try to preempt retaliation.

Unfortunately, since so many important military targets are located in or near cities or urban areas, a 'counter-force' attack against military targets would be equivalent to a full-scale onslaught on most of the cities of the NATO and Warsaw Pact countries. All attempts to study the effects of a full-scale nuclear war are in agreement that a substantial fraction of the world's stockpile of 50,000 nuclear weapons, with a total yield of 13,000–15,000 megatons of explosive power, would be used. The TTAPS group used a figure of 5000 megatons for their baseline study, and also considered the effect of a war in which 10,000 megatons were detonated. The scenario used in the study published in the magazine *Ambio* (the environmental journal of the Royal Swedish Academy of Sciences), involved 5700 megatons. The figure used in calculations at the Lawrence Livermore National Laboratory, California, was 5300 megatons. And the report by the NRC, adopted as their baseline a slightly higher figure, 6500 megatons, which they felt made adequate allowance for weapons which failed to work or which were held in reserve.

Although there is good agreement on the total explosive yield likely to be used in a nuclear war between the superpowers, there are some significant differences between these studies. The TTAPS scientists assumed that weapons with yield up to 10 megatons would be used. The US National Research Council, however, include no weapons larger than 1.5 megatons, pointing out that both the US and the USSR have been increasing the accuracy of their warheads and changing the payloads of their missiles to obtain larger numbers of lower-yield warheads. The advent of cruise missiles has also accelerated the trend towards smaller warheads. The NRC committee express the view that 'by 1985 there will probably be few, if any, multimegaton weapons deployed by either the United States or the Soviet Union, unless present trends are reversed'.

There are also differences in the proportions of weapons assumed to be 'groundbursts' or 'airbursts'. In the TTAPS baseline study, 57 per cent of the bombs were assumed to be groundbursts, though they also studied the effect of varying this proportion between zero and 100 per cent. The NRC committee estimated that only 25 per cent of the bombs would be fused to explode as groundbursts. They arrived at this figure by assuming that weapons were targeted primarily against military targets: missile silos; bases; and command, control, communications and intelligence facilities. As a second priority they assumed that the economic base necessary to sustain military efforts would also be targeted: factories producing military equipment; petroleum refineries and storage; electric power plants; key transport and communication nodes. They assumed that urban areas *per se* would not be targeted and that the type of explosion would be geared to destruction of the military targets rather than to maximize casualties. They therefore assigned one groundburst to each missile silo or other 'hardened' (i.e. strongly protected from the effects of blast with concrete, etc) target.

These somewhat different assumptions by the NRC committee have two consequences. Firstly the smaller number of groundbursts results in a smaller amount of dust being injected into the earth's atmosphere. However, since it was not the dust that played the key role in the nuclear winter effect, this does not change the results very much. Secondly, since it is the groundbursts that are responsible for the main hazard from radioactive fall-out, there may be lower estimates for casualties from fall-out in the NRC scenario than in the TTAPS picture. The NRC committee was not charged with evaluating the biological consequences of a nuclear war, so they did not try to estimate casualties, though they urge that this should now be done using their baseline scenario. The casualties are still likely to be horrendous even with the modified assumptions about the nature of the weapons used.

The NRC committee confirm the claim of the TTAPS group: that the key factor in the nuclear winter effect is the smoke from urban fires and that a much smaller number of warheads targeted against urban areas would have an effect almost as drastic as the full 6500 megaton exchange. The point is that the world's cities can only burn once. The case considered by the TTAPS group was an attack of 1000 weapons each of 100 kilotons yield, 100 megatons in all, directed entirely against targets in urban areas. It is chilling to consider that minor nuclear powers like Britain and France must come close to being able to deliver such an attack.

The NRC committee also considered a more extreme scenario than their baseline, in which an extra 100 20-megaton groundburst explosions are included, bringing the total yield to 8500 megatons. Such weapons might be used in attacks on super-hard targets. The consequence of these additional massive bombs is a far greater yeild of atmospheric dust than in their baseline case.

The amount of dust and smoke generated

The amount of dust swept up in a nuclear explosion depends critically on whether the fireball generated by the explosion touches the ground or not. For a 1-megaton explosion this means that the amount of dust swept up falls off sharply if the detonation altitude is higher than about 2 miles. Airbursts triggered to cause maximum blast damage would therefore sweep up little dust. Estimates of the amount of dust carried up into a stabilized cloud after a groundburst lie in the range 0.2 to 0.5 million tons per megaton of explosive yield and the NRC committee adopt 0.3 million tons per megaton as the most probable value. This agrees exactly with the value adopted by the TTAPS group. The total amount of dust thrown up into the atmosphere is estimated by the NRC committee to lie in the range 330–825 million tons, rather lower than the value of 960 million tons estimated by the TTAPS group, but this is simply a reflection of the lower proportion of groundbursts assumed in the NRC study.

However in the NRC 8500-megaton scenario, an additional 400 to 1000 million tons of dust would be injected into the atmosphere and virtually all of this would be driven straight to the stratosphere.

Estimates of the amount of smoke generated by a full-scale nuclear war are much harder to make. There is no doubt that numerous large-scale fires would be started in a nuclear war. The uncertainties include the areas over which the fires would burn, the amount of combustible material in urban and rural areas, the fraction of this that would be converted to smoke and the speed and extent to which smoke particles are washed out of the nuclear cloud. Paul Crutzen of the Max-Planck-Institute for Chemistry in Mainz, Germany, who first drew the world's attention to the possibility that smoke generated in a nuclear war could have profound climatic consequences, has estimated that 340 million tons of smoke would be produced in the *Ambio* 5700-megaton nuclear war scenario. This is rather higher than the 225 million tons estimated by the TTAPS group in their baseline case. The NRC committee estimated that their baseline scenario of 6500 megatons could yield as much as 180 million tons of smoke, but because of the many uncertainties involved they believe that the plausible range extends from only 20 to as much as 650 million tons of smoke. This is one of the areas in which the NRC committee recommend that intensive research be undertaken, so that a greater understanding of the urban, forest and wild fires likely to be generated in a nuclear war can be obtained. Only at the very lower end of the range of smoke masses given by the NRC committee, say if less than about 50 million tons of smoke were generated, would significant climatic consequences be avoided. Thus very serious consequences can be expected over almost the whole range of values considered plausible by the NRC committee.

How high do the dust and smoke go; how long do they stay up?

In evaluating the likelihood of a nuclear winter we are really only concerned with that part of the dust and smoke that has sizes smaller than 1 micron (one thousandth of a millimetre) since it is these particles that are most effective at absorbing and scattering sunlight.

Even in the early days of atmospheric nuclear testing, samples of bomb debris were collected from the nuclear clouds with both manned and unmanned drone aircraft. The advantage of using unmanned aircraft was that the cloud could be sampled within hours of the explosion. These studies allowed the size distribution of the dust particles swept up into the atmosphere in a nuclear explosion to be measured. A typical value for the fraction of the dust in a stabilized nuclear cloud which is in the form of particles smaller than 1 micron in radius is 8 per cent. This is the value quoted by the NRC committee and it happens to be the same as that used in the TTAPS study. The NRC committee quote a range of from a few per cent to 20 per cent for this proportion.

The sizes of the particles in a smoke cloud depend on what is being burnt and what type of fire is burning it. Most sooty smokes consist of very small (less than one-fiftieth of a micron in radius) graphite crystals and varying amounts of oils and tars. In dry smokes the carbon crystals coagulate into chain structures with dimensions of about one-tenth of a micron. In oily smoke, droplets of heavy organic liquids laced with soot particles can grow to sizes of 0.2 microns or more. In forest fires the majority of the smoke particles are found to be smaller than a micron in size, and the same will probably be true for urban fires. However there are several effects which tend to change the distribution of particle sizes in a smoke plume. Soot particles tend to coagulate together and so the average size of smoke particles grows with time. Nevertheless it is not thought that this growth will take the particles over the critical one micron size. The characteristic smoke particle size adopted by the NRC committee was one-tenth of a micron. A second effect is that water droplets and ice crystals forming in a rising smoke plume tend to collect up soot and charcoal particles, in a process known as 'scavenging'. These then fall to the ground as a 'black rain', a phenomenon which was noticed at Hiroshima and Nagasaki. Even if the water droplets evaporate again within the cloud, the soot particles will have been aggregated together and the size distribution of the smoke particles will have changed. However black rain is not seen associated with forest fires and this scavenging process may not be very efficient at removing smoke particles smaller than 1 micron anyway. For their baseline calculation the NRC committee assume that 50 per cent of the smoke from nuclear fires is immediately removed as black rain and state that they regard this as a conservative assumption.

The height to which the smoke and dust are driven has a critical effect on how long the nuclear winter lasts. Particles that reach the stratosphere (an altitude of about 8 miles under normal mid-latitude atmospheric conditions) are no longer subject to being washed out by rainfall and so drift down very slowly under gravity. A particle of radius 1 micron would take about a month to drift down, while a particle of one-tenth of a micron would take a year or so.

The TTAPS group estimated that 80 per cent of the sub-micron dust injected into the atmosphere in nuclear explosions would reach the stratosphere, whereas the NRC committee estimate was just under 40 per cent. This is just a reflection of the fact that the NRC baseline study includes no weapons with explosive yield greater that 1.5 megatons, whereas the TTAPS baseline case has weapons of up to 10 megatons. The larger weapons are much more effective at lofting dust into the stratosphere. Since the NRC baseline has so many fewer groundbursts, so that the total amount of dust ejected is lower than the TTAPS estimate, the NRC committee estimate for the amount of stratospheric dust smaller than 1 micron in size is only 10–23 million tons, compared with 65 million tons assumed in the TTAPS study. However, in the extreme case considered by the NRC committee in which an additional 100 20-megaton weapons are detonated against super-hard targets, a further 30–80 million tons of sub-micron sized dust would be injected into the stratosphere.

The height to which smoke plumes rise has been measured in both forest and urban fires. The plumes from forest fires can often reach to altitudes of 4 miles or more. Intense urban fires would be expected to rise to even higher altitudes. The NRC committee assumed that the smoke from nuclear fires would be spread more or less uniformly up to an altitude of about 6 miles. Only under exceptional conditions do they expect that even a massive city fire would inject smoke into the stratosphere. The TTAPS group assumed that forest-fire plumes would extend to an altitude of 4 miles, that urban fires would extend up to 5 miles, and that 5 per cent of urban fires would develop firestorm conditions in which the smoke would be driven to altitudes of up to 12 miles.

A crucial step in the calculation of how long the nuclear winter lasts is to estimate how much of the smoke and dust are washed out by rain. The TTAPS group assume that this occurs throughout the lower atmosphere (troposphere), to an altitude of 8 miles, at a rate that declines with increasing altitude. Above the tropopause, in the stratosphere, where rain clouds rarely form, no washout is assumed to take place. This calculation fails to take account of the modification of the atmospheric temperature profile brought about by the nuclear cloud of dust and smoke. The heating of the upper atmosphere by the dust, as the latter absorbs the sun's radiation, brings the temperature inversion which defines the junction between the troposphere and the stratosphere down to a much lower altitude. This means that dust and smoke above an altitude of 3 miles are not likely to be washed out by rain. The NRC committee therefore incorporate this change into their calculation, but they also adopt a rather higher washout rate than the TTAPS group at the lower altitudes. The NRC committee have also calculated a 'fast-rainout' case in which they set the rate at which dust and smoke are washed out to the highest value they consider reasonable.

To evaluate the effects of the cloud of dust and smoke it is now necessary to estimate the absorbing and scattering properties of the dust and smoke particles. While the values adopted by the NRC committee are very similar to those used by the TTAPS group, the NRC committee point out that their assumed values could be in error by a factor of 2 to 3. However, even if the particles are less efficient absorbers and scatterers by this amount, the nuclear winter effect would not disappear unless the amount of smoke injected into the atmosphere were well below their baseline assumption.

With the baseline assumptions made about the amount of dust and smoke, its distribution through the atmosphere, the rate of washout, and the properties of the particles, the NRC committee then calculate the temperature that would be expected at ground level in a continental interior at different times after a nuclear war, ignoring the effects of winds and oceans. Assuming that the dust remains confined to the latitudes 30–70 degrees North where most of the bombs are expected to be detonated, and that the dust is spread around uniformly in longitude within this band, they calculate that the temperature would drop by 31 °C (56 °F) for about 25 days and that it would take 76 days for this temperature to be reduced by half. If the dust and smoke were spread over the whole northern hemisphere, the temperature would drop by 21 °C (38 °F) for about 17 days, taking 51 days for the temperature drop to be reduced by half. Although not quite as severe as the TTAPS group's baseline case, these values confirm the phenomenon of the nuclear winter – months of very severely reduced temperatures. Bear in mind that the lost summer of 1816 involved an average temperature reduction of only 3 °C (5 °F) for 3 months.

How uniformly does the dust and smoke spread out?

The area initially covered by smoke plumes would depend on the number of fires, their sizes and duration, the average wind speed and whether the wind direction is variable. For major urban fires with plumes extending upwards through a substantial fraction of the troposphere, the high winds at these altitudes would produce plumes several hundred miles in length. It is reasonable to suppose that substantial fractions of Eurasia and North America would be covered initially by smoke plumes. Local wind systems would develop which would tend to smooth out irregularities in the smoke coverage within the first two days, and after about three days the major gap over the North Atlantic would be likely to have been filled. A calculation carried out at Oregon State University using a three-dimensional computer simulation of the global atmosphere showed that after three days most of Russia, Europe, North Africa and North America are covered in a continuous cloud of smoke and dust. For over 20 per cent of the northern hemisphere the intensity of sunlight is reduced to less than 1 per cent of normal, and there are several very large patches of a million square miles or more where the sunlight intensity is down to less than a hundred-millionth of normal, in other words to pitch darkness. Under these patches the temperature drop will be very much more severe than the average values quoted above.

Whether the dust and smoke spread to the southern hemisphere is an issue that has not yet been resolved. There are several indications that the modifications of atmospheric circulation brought about by the dust and smoke cloud would favour the transport of smoke and dust to the southern hemisphere. Interhemispheric transport of dust has been observed following volcanic eruptions, though this is probably only the dust that reaches the stratosphere. The stratospheric dust generated in a nuclear war would not, in the baseline case, be capable of causing drastic climatic change on its own. A more reliable estimate of the fate of the southern hemisphere after a nuclear war can only be made when three-dimensional computer simulations of the atmosphere are able to follow the evolution of the dust and smoke cloud for some months after the catastrophe.

Nuclear winter weather

We saw in Chapter 3 that the effect of the world's weather, particularly winds blowing from the warmer oceans across the freezing continents, is to reduce the severity of the temperature drop after a nuclear war. Very cold temperatures are still expected in the continental interiors of Asia and North America, but coastal regions like Western Europe and California may not have nearly so bad a time.

How certain are these detailed atmospheric simulations and is it possible that the climatic consequences are much less severe or much worse than predicted at the moment? It has to be said that the three-dimensional computer simulations of the global atmosphere are crude in several respects. Most are not able to follow the effects of winds and atmospheric circulation on the dust and smoke cloud. They are not able to include the detailed processes like coagulation and washout which tend to remove dust from the atmosphere. They neglect the cooling of the oceans and the oceanic circulation. Infrared radiation from the dust and smoke particles and scattering of sunlight are also neglected. So far there has been little investigation of how the climatic consequences of a nuclear war depend on the season in which the war takes place.

However it does not seem likely, in my opinion, that these effects will drastically alter the conclusions of the simulations. Although it is clear that much work remains to be done to understand accurately the nuclear winter effect, the main uncertainties lie in the amount of smoke generated and in how rapidly it is removed from the atmosphere, rather than in the computer simulations.

Will there be a nuclear winter and is it a crisis for life on earth?

Finally we have to ask the question: given all the uncertainties discussed here, is it still possible to say that a nuclear war is likely to be followed by a nuclear winter? To try to answer this I have drawn up a table of what, according to the US National Research Council committee on 'The Effects on the Atmosphere of a Major Nuclear Exchange', are possible outcomes of a nuclear war. I have indicated the approximate severity of the different cases compared to the NRC committee's baseline: this factor can be taken to give the amount of smoke generated in a nuclear war, though there are other factors which have a similar effect (e.g. the absorbing efficiency of the smoke particles). How long the smoke stays in the atmosphere is another crucial factor in the severity of the nuclear winter effect. Rather than try to show all the possible combinations of smoke-cloud lifetime and smoke-cloud mass, I have shown the smoke lifetime increasing from the least severe to the most severe cases. The typical temperature drops for northern hemisphere locations are very approximate, and for some of the cases are just 'guesstimates'. In assessing the biological consequences of the different cases, a major problem is that the panel of biologists at the 1983 Washington conference decided to investigate the most extreme case, and it is not easy to extrapolate their conclusions to the less severe cases.

Case	A	B	C	D	E
Severity (compared to NRC baseline)	× 1/4	× 1/2	× 1	× 2	× 4
By whom investigated			NRC baseline US (NCAR) 3-D model	TTAPS baseline	TTAPS extreme Soviet 3-D model
Typical temperature drop (N. hemisphere)	Few °C	5–20 °C (9–36 °F)	10–25 °C (18–45 °F)	15–30 °C (27–54 °F)	25–40 °C (45–72 °F)
Duration of cold spell	1 week– 1 month		1–3 months		1 year
Biological consequences	Minor	Serious	Serious	Severe	Catastrophic
Extinctions	None	Some possible	Some	Widespread	Major extinction event
World harvest	Damaged	Lost	Lost	Lost	Lost
Consequence for humans	Economic problems for poorer nations	Serious threat to war survivors, serious problems for noncombatants		Severe crisis worldwide, survival not certain	

To summarise, it is possible within the existing uncertainties that the climatic consequences of a nuclear war would be fairly minor, comparable to the lost summer of 1816. It is equally possible that the consequences are so severe that a major extinction event will occur and that survival of the human race is in doubt. The TTAPS group took as their baseline a case rather more severe than the NRC committee considered most probable, though the latter may have erred on the side of underestimating the effects in order to add credibility to their report and avoid any possible accusations of exaggeration. For the complacency of Edward Teller and John Maddox to be justified, one or more of the predicted quantities must lie right at the bottom end of what is considered plausible. At the present state of our scientific knowledge we cannot say which of these five cases is correct, but our ignorance is such that I would be justified in claiming that all are equally likely. Thus a 20 per cent chance of there being virtually no climatic change after a nuclear war has to be balanced against a 20 per cent chance of a major extinction event, perhaps including *homo sapiens* amongst the victims. The probability of a severe nuclear winter effect seems high.

Chapter 6

What is going through the minds of the nuclear strategists?

The unthinkable calculations

Many of us find it very hard to imagine how an intelligent human being can bear to perform the kind of calculations the nuclear strategists go in for. A horrifying glimpse of the megadeath mentality was given as far back as 1960 in Herman Kahn's book *On Thermonuclear War*. There he writes about the destruction of the 50 largest cities and towns of the United States, and the death of one-third of the US population, as being the type of loss that the victor might have to tolerate in a nuclear war. In that book too we read for the first time of 'first strike' and 'counterforce' strategies and began to see that to the nuclear strategists a nuclear war is simply a game of chess.

Twenty-five years later the game still continues, with the new accurate missiles making a first strike, counterforce strategy an attractive choice. The calculations show that even in an all-out nuclear war, where a large proportion of the world's nuclear arsenals are detonated, between a third and a half of the populations of the United States and of the Soviet Union would survive the immediate effects of the war. Amongst these survivors would be the nuclear strategists themselves, deep in their command-post bunkers, safe even from a direct hit. According to the pre-nuclear winter calculations they have only to lie low for a few weeks until the radioactivity levels have fallen to a 'safe' level before emerging to organize post-nuclear society and start rebuilding the nuclear arsenals.

The military-industrial complex

When he left office in 1961, President Eisenhower warned of the immensely powerful lobby that had grown up consisting of the weapons manufacturers and their military customers. So vast and powerful had this military-industrial complex become that it was becoming almost impossible for the transient politicians to keep control of it.

When we look at the number of nuclear bombs in the arsenals of the superpowers today, together with the missiles, bombers, ships and submarines which can deliver them to a target, we can immediately get an idea of the vast industrial forces needed to build and maintain these arsenals. The vested interest involved in maintaining a nuclear strategy and in continuing the escalation of the arms race appears immovable. This is a vested interest that will be extremely reluctant to accept the nuclear winter calculations; that will doubt-less produce its own version of the calculations with a bias towards the less severe end of the uncertainty range; and that will resist to the end efforts to reduce the arsenals and move away from a nuclear strategy. This has been exactly the response of the US Depart-ment of Defense to the report by the US National

Research Council on the climatic effects of nuclear war. In a report to the US Congress in March 1985, the US Secretary of Defense acknowledges the possibility of severe climatic change following a nuclear war, but places great emphasis on the uncertainties in the nuclear winter calculations and denies that any change of policy is required.

Even so, the politicians, defence experts and military strategists are taking the nuclear winter predictions very seriously. In 1984 President Reagan announced that 50 million dollars was being made available for research into the atmospheric consequences of nuclear war. In the United States we see many scientists and powerful computing resources being brought to bear on the problem and it is clear that serious studies are being undertaken too in the Soviet Union. In Britain, however, the Defence Minister, Michael Heseltine, is reported as regarding the nuclear winter effect as of little importance and merely having the effect of enhancing the strength of nuclear deterrence. The pronouncements of the British Home Office about civil defence in a nuclear war and of the Ministry of Defence about nuclear strategy make one seriously wonder whether Britain is actually competent to be a nuclear power. This is particularly so given that the British arsenal is almost large enough, if directed at cities (and where else would Britain's small force be directed?), to trigger a nuclear winter.

The impact of the nuclear winter on nuclear strategy

What is the effect of the nuclear winter predictions on

nuclear strategy likely to be? For although we can not expect an immediate *volte-face* by the superpowers, the impact of these predictions on their thinking is likely to be enormous. For European countries the impact is perhaps less, because these nations are already resigned to enormous casualties in the event of an all-out nuclear war. The temperature drops predicted for much of Europe are considerably less severe than for the continental interiors of the United States and the Soviet Union, so the nuclear winter makes the prospect of a nuclear war only marginally worse. As Tony Hart, member of the Greater London Council and of the British organization SANA (Scientists Against Nuclear Arms) has remarked, 'the Nuclear Winter is an irrelevance – what happens to plants after we're dead'.

For the superpowers the situation looks very different though. Suddenly they are faced with the prospect that has loomed over Europe for decades – the possible destruction of the vast majority of their populations. Even the nuclear strategists themselves might not survive the more extreme nuclear winter scenarios.

Is there anything they can do which would eliminate the threat of a nuclear winter without reducing their beloved nuclear arsenals? At first sight the current trend towards lower yield weapons is a move in the right direction, since the amount of dust ejected to high altitudes is greatly reduced. However, the nuclear winter effect is mainly dependent on the smoke generated in urban fires and a greater number of smaller weapons would probably be even more effective at starting conflagrations than the current arsenals. A ban on nuclear weapons against cities is what would be needed but this is hopelessly unrealistic given the concentration of key military targets in or near urban areas. Moreover, as Carl Sagan has pointed out, when the superpowers cannot even agree to methods of verifying the number of missiles each side possesses, there is certainly no way to verify the targets of the missiles, encoded in a minute silicon chip.

Other possible strategies discussed by Sagan in an article in the magazine *Foreign Affairs* in June 1984, are a sub-threshold first strike, hoping that the victim will not dare to retaliate for fear of triggering a nuclear winter (this is unlikely to be effective at 'taking out' the opposition's land-based arsenal and is useless against submarines) and a move towards high-accuracy, low-yield, earth-burrowing warheads. The latter would be ideal for 'taking out' military bases and command bunkers without causing fall-out or a nuclear winter, but again is useless against submarines.

To eliminate the risk of a nuclear winter, there are several immediate steps that must be taken by the superpowers:

i) Reduce the risk of a nuclear war starting accidentally by declaring that neither side intends to be the first to use nuclear weapons. It is especially crucial that NATO move away from its strategy of a first strike with tactical nuclear weapons in response to a conventional attack by Warsaw pact countries.

ii) Abandon any intention to move towards a 'launch on warning' strategy, in which a computer detecting a missile attack through early-warning radar systems is programmed to initiate a nuclear counter-attack.

iii) Freeze the nuclear arsenals at their present level immediately.

iv) Move towards massive reductions in the nuclear arsenals, until they are below the threshold at which a nuclear winter can be caused. Even 10 or 50 1-megaton bombs constitutes a perfectly adequate nuclear deterrent, and it is a madness that the superpowers have the equivalent of over 5000 each.

Without these moves the future of the human species is very bleak indeed. And is it absurdly unrealistic and idealistic to hope that nuclear weapons should ultimately be banned completely?

Chapter 7

Scientists and the nuclear winter

The tragic story of the birth of nuclear weapons

I have already described how the discovery of the nuclear winter effect has drawn scientists from many different fields and from many countries into the debate. Some have turned from their normal research to work more or less full-time on the nuclear winter problems. Many others have brought their expertise to bear on those parts of the enormously complex calculation that they can help with. To understand why the nuclear winter has become so important to these scientists we have to look back to the birth of nuclear weapons and to understand the feeling of guilt that many scientists feel about this nuclear age.

The possibility that the enormous energy of the atomic nucleus might be used to construct a bomb began to be speculated about in the early 1930s, though many eminent physicists ridiculed the idea. As early as 1935 the Hungarian physicist Leo Szilard, then working in Berlin, approached a number of fellow atomic scientists to ask whether it might be advisable to consider refraining from publishing the results of their investigations. This suggestion was not taken seriously at the time. Early in 1939, as a result of work in France and Germany, the break-up or fission of the uranium atom into atoms of the element barium began to be understood and this heralded the dawn of the nuclear age. Leo Szilard, who had emigrated to New York, became increasingly worried about the possibility of a chain reaction, in which a uranium atom splits and emits some high energy neutrons which then split other uranium atoms in an escalating chain. This could be used to manufacture a bomb of unprecedented power. He renewed his efforts to persuade physicists to impose a voluntary censorship on their work. By one of the ironies of history one of the three colleagues who joined him in this campaign was Edward Teller. This time the campaign did find favour amongst American physicists. Unfortunately the French physicist Frederic Joliot-Curie was about to publish the discovery by himself and his colleagues of the chain reaction. So keen was he to have the credit for this discovery that the paper was sent to the London magazine *Nature*, which publishes papers faster than most other scientific journals. The manuscript was even taken in person by one of Joliot-Curie's colleagues to Le Bourget airport to be placed in the London mailbag and was published only ten days later on 18 March 1939. This action was to sabotage Szilard's campaign.

The possibility that the Nazis might try to construct an atom bomb filled the American physicists with alarm. Several of the greatest atomic physicists of the day, like Werner Heisenberg and Otto Hahn, were still living in Germany and they had the expertise to build an atom bomb, if such a thing were possible. Szilard decided that he should try to alert the US Government to this danger. Because he was himself almost unknown in the United States, he persuaded Einstein to sign a letter to President Roosevelt which called amongst other things for an acceleration of atomic research. Einstein, who had devoted much of his life to campaigning for international peace, was later horrified to realize that he had given the starting signal for the development of the atom bomb.

As it happened, the fears of the American physicists about developments in Germany were unjustified. Hitler took little interest in scientific research and had already driven into exile many of the best scientists of the day. More importantly the key German physicists like Heisenberg were determined that Hitler should not have an atom bomb. Although they continued to work on uranium and the chain reaction, they successfully kept the German Government in the dark about the possibility of a bomb. This passive resistance by the German scientists is one of the more dignified episodes in the history of the birth of nuclear weapons. Heisenberg has remarked that 'In the summer of 1939 twelve people might still have been able, by coming to mutual agreement, to prevent the construction of atom bombs.' An opportunity to forge such an agreement did in fact come in the summer of 1939 when Heisenberg visited the United States, but perhaps the atmosphere of mutual suspicion was already too great.

One last opportunity to halt the development of the atom bomb occurred in October 1941, when Heisenberg gave a lecture in occupied Copenhagen and took the opportunity to visit his old teacher and friend Niels Bohr, who was in touch with atomic physicists in Britain and the United States. Heisenberg wanted to convey to Bohr that the German physicists did not intend to allow Hitler to have an atom bomb but he knew that Bohr was under German surveillance and could not bring himself to be frank. When Bohr asked Heisenberg if he thought a bomb were technically feasible, Heisenberg replied that he knew that it was but that it would require enormous technical effort. This conveyed to Bohr exactly the opposite of what he intended– that a major effort was under way in Germany to construct a bomb.

The letter composed by Szilard and signed by Einstein did not reach President Roosevelt till October 1939. Although Roosevelt was interested it took enormous efforts by Szilard and his colleagues to get the project off the ground. It was not till 6 December 1941, just one day before the Japanese attack on Pearl Harbor, that a decision was taken to put substantial financial and technical resources into the construction of the atom bomb. At first the Manhattan Project, as it was called, consisted of a series of parallel efforts in laboratories throughout the United States, Britain and Canada. Robert Oppenheimer, who started to work full-time on the project at Berkeley, California, early in 1942, suggested that a group of laboratories should be established at one location and this idea found considerable support. Work on a remote desert site near Los Alamos, New Mexico, began in November 1942 and by July 1943 the scientists were assembled and Oppenheimer had been appointed director of the Los Alamos laboratory. Two years later the scientists of Los Alamos were ready to test the first atomic bomb.

By this time the war with Germany was over, so the original reason for having the atom bomb had disappeared. The target for the bomb was now the Japanese cities and a shortlist of four had been drawn up by a committee consisting mainly of Los Alamos scientists. At this point it would have again been possible for the scientists to influence the course of events by advising that the bomb should be exploded in a demonstration to the Japanese rather than directly on their cities. This was the proposal advocated by a committee of seven scientists set up at the University of Chicago under the chairmanship of the Nobel prize winner James Franck, and including Leo Szilard, in a report sent to the US Secretary of War in June 1945. This far-seeing report predicted that there would be a nuclear arms race in the post-war period if international agreement were not reached swiftly. But the scientists, including Oppenheimer, who were advising the new American President, Harry Truman, did not support the initiative of the Franck report. Hiroshima and Nagasaki were doomed.

During the years after the war many American scientists campaigned for civilian control of atomic research and against any build-up of atomic weapons. Unfortunately the American public were in no mood to respond to such a campaign. The testing and production of atom bombs soon resumed. In August 1949 a US Air Force 'flying laboratory' discovered traces of radioactive material in the atmosphere. It was soon realized that the Soviet Union had successfully tested an atom bomb. Soon afterwards Edward Teller's long campaign for work on a 'super' bomb, the hydrogen bomb, met with presidential approval. In November 1952 the first hydrogen bomb was exploded in the Marshall Islands in the South Pacific, to be followed by the first Soviet H-bomb test only nine months later.

There was to be no turning back from the nuclear arms race.

Looking back over this tragic story, we see that there were many opportunities to escape from the arms race. At every stage, from 1935 onwards, there were individuals who gave clear warnings of what the future held. Yet nuclear weapons were not manufactured by the military in the face of opposition from the scientists at this misuse of their knowledge. The scientists themselves pressed for the programme to develop the weapons to be started, built them with great energy and enthusiasm, selected the targets, and advised that the bombs should be used.

Perhaps it is too easy to argue with hindsight. The actions of Szilard and Einstein in pressing for development of the atom bomb as a defensive measure against Nazism are understandable. It is also understandable that the atomic scientists, many of whom had seen Nazism at close quarters, should be eager to work to overthrow Hitler. If I had been in their position, I would probably have agreed to work on the Manhattan Project. But history will never forgive the decision to use the atom bomb against Japanese cities.

It has been argued that only three atom bombs were available at the time and that if a demonstration explosion failed, the opportunity to end the war in Japan swiftly would have been lost. But such a risk of failure applied even more strongly to the two bombs transported to the Pacific and dropped on Japan. This risk-of-failure argument is hard to accept. The scientists knew that the atom bomb worked even better than they had expected. The reality, surely, is that the military and many of the scientists wanted to test the bomb on a real target. Why, otherwise, after the devastating results of the Hiroshima explosion, did a second bomb have to be dropped on Nagasaki three days later, primed to explode at a different altitude from the Hiroshima bomb? This has all the hallmarks of a ghastly scientific experiment.

Bethe's calculation

In the early stages of the Manhattan Project an anxiety suddenly grew amongst the scientists that detonation of an atomic bomb might start a chain reaction which would engulf the whole earth in one vast nuclear explosion. Hans Bethe was entrusted with the task of calculating whether this was a real possibility. He found that this would not happen and so the project continued.

The nuclear winter calculation is rather analagous to Bethe's calculation. Naturally there have been several investigations over the years to evaluate whether a nuclear war would have catastrophic long-term effects on the earth. These have always concluded, up to now, that there are no such effects. The world's arsenal of nuclear weapons passed the threshold for causing a serious nuclear winter effect as long ago as 1953. It is strange that it has taken us 30 years to realize the severity of the climatic consequences of a nuclear war. It is tragic for humanity too since if we had realized this 30 years ago, the insane nuclear arms race might have been prevented.

Reagan's star wars scenario

Since it seems to be so hard to control the growth of the

nuclear arsenals, is there any hope that an effective defence against nuclear weapons can be devised? This is the hope that lies behind President Reagan's 'Strategic Defence Initiative'. In the 1983 speech in which he launched this initiative, he called on the United States' scientific community 'to give us the means of rendering these nuclear weapons impotent and obsolete' by finding methods to intercept and destroy ballistic missiles before they reach their targets.

The search for a defence against ballistic missiles carrying nuclear warheads began in the 1960s when the two superpowers developed anti-ballistic-missiles (ABM) systems based on the use of an interceptor missile armed with a nuclear warhead. In 1968 the USSR began to operate an ABM system around Moscow and by 1974 the US had completed a similar system to protect Minuteman missiles near Grand Forks Air Force base in North Dakota. The problem with these systems was that they were vulnerable to deception by decoys and they led directly to the development of MIRVs – multiple independently targetable re-entry vehicles. Each missile, instead of carrying a single weapon, was designed to carry several missiles along with a variety of devices to help them deceive the opposition's radar and ABM systems – for example light-weight decoys, weapons camouflaged to resemble decoys, radar-reflecting wires called 'chaff' and infrared-emitting aerosols.

In the late 1960s several scientists who had been involved in investigating ABM systems as advisers to the US government took the unusual step of publicly airing their criticisms of the proposed ABM systems.

Many scientists took part in the ensuing debate and a consensus emerged about the flaws in the proposed ABM systems. They were too vulnerable to deception and other countermeasures and, anyway, the Soviet Union could simply increase the number of missiles used in an attack until the ABM system was saturated. These arguments carried the day and in May 1972 a treaty was signed in Moscow by President Nixon and General-Secretary Brezhnev banning ABM systems. The MIRVs ought to have been banned along with the ABM systems, but unfortunately, despite the warnings of scientific advisers that they would undermine the strategic balance between the superpowers, the US pressed ahead with their development. The USSR soon followed. The massive increase in the number of nuclear warheads in both strategic arsenals during the 1970s can be largely attributed to the introduction of MIRVs.

Reagan's Strategic Defence Initiative calls for protection of the entire United States from missile attack. This means that virtually every one of the 10,000 or so nuclear warheads that the Soviet Union can commit to an attack must be intercepted and destroyed. Because of the elaborate deception that a MIRVed missile can practice, creating a vast 'threat cloud' of weapons, decoys and chaff, it is essential that the majority of the missiles be destroyed soon after they are launched. This has to be done while the booster rockets are still firing, before the MIRV system (known as a 'bus') starts to send its various passengers off on their different orbits. At present, booster rockets continue firing only during the first few minutes after launch and it is possible in the near future that this period could be reduced to only 100 seconds. At this point in their orbit, the Soviet missiles are not visible from any point on the earth's surface accessible to NATO, so the attack can only be made from space. Hence the nickname 'Star Wars' for Reagan's plan.

The interceptors would have to be either permanently in orbit, in which case many would be needed to achieve continuous surveillance of the Soviet Union, or could be 'pop-up' systems launched by submarines when there is a threat of attack. The destruction of the missiles would be by some kind of projectile homing in on the infrared radiation from the missile's exhaust, or by more exotic devices like X-ray lasers or high-energy particle beams. However, these systems would take several decades to develop, will cost enormous sums of money and, most important of all, have little prospect of being completely effective. Some of the objections that have been raised are: (1) since offensive weapons are likely to be cheaper than the proposed defensive ones, any defence system can be overwhelmed by a missile build-up, (2) the defence would have to attack every object that behaved like a booster rocket, (3) the space-based interceptors will be far more vulnerable to attack than the ICBMs they are intended to destroy, (4) schemes based on infrared detection of boosters are vulnerable to deception.

The feasibility of Reagan's proposal has been attacked on all sides. We have to hope that these arguments will eventually prevail and that there will be a new agreement between the US and the USSR banning the militarization of space. I do not believe that anti-missile defence offers any real hope of protecting us from the consequences of a nuclear war and I hope that scientists will resolutely resist the calls of Ronald Reagan and Margaret Thatcher to work on these systems.

How the military use the scientists

It is clear that scientists bear a heavy burden of responsibility for the invention of the atom bomb during the Second World War, its use against the Japanese cities of Hiroshima and Nagasaki, and the subsequent development of the hydrogen bomb during peace time. Science continues to be heavily involved in the nuclear weapons industry today, with many scientists working on building, testing and improving nuclear weapons and the missile systems to deliver them. It has been estimated that as many as 40 per cent of physics graduates at British and American universities end up working for the defence industry in some form or other.

There are some subtler ways that science is used by the military establishment. Astronomy ought to be as far as one could get from involvement in military research. Yet it is used to provide window-dressing for the space programme and the space programme in turn is used to lend respectability to the development of ever larger and more accurate missiles, let alone the increasing militarization of space. The space shuttle is a good example of a project which could never have survived if it was not needed by the military.

I have just spent several years of my life involved with a space astronomy project called the Infrared Astronomical Satellite, IRAS for short, whose purpose was to make a survey of the sky at infrared wavelengths. On several occasions I became aware of how this project was being subtly used by the military and its allies. IRAS had to be launched from Vandenberg Air Force Base in California, because it had to go into a polar orbit, in order to achieve its surveillance of the sky. 'Air Force Base' is a euphemism of course: this is in fact a missile base. Enormous efforts were made to get press and media coverage of the launch and, sure enough, all the TV news programmes showed beautiful pictures of the IRAS launch, giving Vandenberg 'Air Force' Base just the type of clean, healthy publicity it needs. A demonstration taking place at the gates of the base against the proposed deployment of MX missiles did not achieve quite as much publicity. Soon after the successful launch of the satellite and ejection of the telescope cover, the contractors who had made the cryostat and the telescope, Ball Brothers, proudly announced in *Aviation Week* that they now confidently expected large orders for military infrared satellites. And after a few months of the mission the scientists were subjected to enormous pressure from NASA to give a large-scale presentation of IRAS results to the US Congress, to help bolster NASA's budget submission (the shuttle programme was not going too well at the time).

In a letter written some months before he died, Martin Ryle, the pioneer radio-astronomer and Nobel Prize winner for Physics, wrote that after the Second World War he had looked around for a subject far removed from military applications and had chosen astronomy. By the end of his life, however, the developments in radio detection techniques he had pioneered had become of the greatest interest to the military and he began to wonder whether it would not have been better if he had become a farmer in 1946. He also asked the question whether it may not be time to stop research in fundamental science now, before new horrors are invented. These are sombre thoughts from someone who devoted most of his life to scientific research. It was Martin Ryle who helped to show that the British nuclear power industry acts as an important source of plutonium for UK and US nuclear weapons and he spent the last decade of his life campaigning against nuclear weapons and the nuclear power industry.

I think that scientists from all areas of science would be able to add to these anecdotes of how the military-industrial complex use science, either directly or indirectly. The scientists who take a stand on these issues are, unfortunately, only a minority. Most feel that political issues should be left to others to decide and that they have no personal responsibility for how science is used.

I have said that I think scientists must accept responsibility for the development of nuclear weapons. It was scientists who pushed for the atom bomb to be developed, who built it with great energy, who advised that it be dropped on Japanese cities, and who pushed for the development of the even more destructive hydrogen bomb. The person in the street knew nothing of these developments at the time and today continues to be deceived into acquiescence or support for the nuclear arms race. I feel that scientists have a duty to campaign against nuclear weapons, for example through organisations like Scientists Against Nuclear Arms (SANA) in Britain and the Union of

Concerned Scientists in the United States. This is a duty that we scientists owe to our fellow human beings.

The nuclear winter effect offers scientists a unique opportunity. If the predictions are correct then the present nuclear strategies have to change; the current vast arsenals have to be reduced drastically. There is even the possibility that the world may be persuaded to renounce nuclear weapons completely. I hope that more and more scientists from the many disciplines that can contribute to the nuclear winter debate will become involved. At present the demonstrable possibility that a nuclear war would cause a major extinction event on the earth and that the human species might well be among the victims gives us an opportunity to force governments back from the brink. In the end, though, everything will depend on ordinary people refusing to support nuclear weapons any more.

Possible Futures

There are two images of the future that come to me. One is that at some moment during the next century, and sooner rather than later, intelligent life in the universe might cease. For there is no evidence for other life in the universe and no guarantee that life will ever develop in any other place but this. A nuclear war would not end life on earth, however extreme the nuclear winter. For deep in the oceans, around the fumaroles of underwater volcanoes, there are organisms which do not depend on solar energy at all. The catastrophe that put an end to the dinosaurs, perhaps very similar to the extreme nuclear winter scenario, only killed off half of the species then alive. Life will go on, but without us.

The second image is that on some day millions of years in the future some other civilization stumbles on the earth and all its marvellous life and finds the relics of our own brief civilization, like the archeologists stumbling on the tomb of Tutenkamen. This is only slightly more comforting than the first image.

Even if it turns out that the climatic consequences of a nuclear war can be shown to be minor, the direct consequences of nuclear war are so appalling that humanity must draw back from this abyss. The nuclear winter magnifies the consequences and compels immediate action. We cannot let human existence on this beautiful planet be snuffed out.

A simplified calculation of how cold the earth gets in the nuclear winter

The flow of radiation through a cloud of dust or smoke is a complex phenomenon, which can only be studied properly with elaborate computer programmes run on very big computers. Several critics of the nuclear winter have claimed that even if a thick cloud of dust and smoke shrouds the earth, the net effect at ground level could be a heating of the earth rather than a cooling. This is because the ground temperature is controlled not only by the amount of solar radiation reaching the ground but also by the heating of air molecules (the greenhouse effect) and of the dust and smoke particles. In addition, the main heat loss from the ground in the tropics is by convection of the atmosphere rather than by direct radiation, which enormously complicates the calculation.

Although there is no real alternative to doing these detailed calculations with a big computer, I thought it might be useful to give a highly simplified version of the calculations. This simplified version gives answers very similar to the detailed calculations and shows that if a shroud of small dust and smoke particles forms, a cooling is inevitable outside the tropics. I will also in passing mention the case of volcanic dust veils.

The assumptions

To start with I am going to neglect the processes (e.g. absorption and scattering by ozone molecules) which prevent some of the sun's radiation from reaching the ground even on a clear, sunny day. I shall just assume this lost radiation was never there to start with. Next I shall assume that the ground radiates away all the energy it receives and that the ground temperature is given by Stefan's law for a perfect radiator (p.39). This means that for the moment I am neglecting the vertical convection of heat in the atmosphere, so the calculation is relevant to mid-latitudes only. It also means I am neglecting for the moment the fact that some sunlight is reflected away by the ground (typically about 10–15 per cent of the total) and that I am assuming that the energy absorbed by growing plants is balanced by the energy released by dying plants and by animals. I will also neglect the horizontal advection of heat by winds and oceans, so that the calculation is relevant to a continental interior, but not to a coastal location. Next I will assume that the total rate of flow of radiant energy (visible plus infrared), either upwards of downwards, is the same at all levels in the earth's atmosphere. This neglects the fact that some of the energy absorbed by the earth's atmosphere is used to drive the weather rather than being re-radiated. Next I assume that when an absorbing layer like the earth's atmosphere or the nuclear cloud of dust and smoke absorbs energy (either from above or below) it re-radiates equal amounts of energy upwards and downwards. This is valid for a layer which does not absorb very strongly and for a strongly absorbing layer if the temperature is constant through the layer. However, it may not be a very good approximation in all cases. Finally I am going to simplify enormously the calculation by assuming that there are just two types of radiation involved, visible light and infrared radiation (radiant heat), and I am going to neglect the fact that, for example, visible light consists of radiation of many different wavelengths (red, blue etc) and that absorbing particles absorb radiation of different wavelengths with differing efficiencies. I shall assume that air molecules absorb negligible amounts of visible light, and that dust and smoke particles absorb negligible amounts of infrared radiation (by comparison with air molecules anyway), which should be valid if the particles are small.

I will now show how with these assumptions the temperature of the ground can be calculated for different cases:

Case A   Earth with no atmosphere

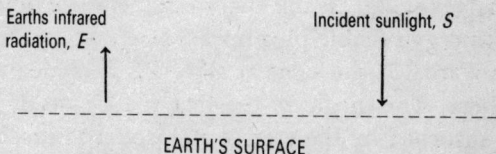

Earths infrared radiation, E ↑   Incident sunlight, S ↓

- -

EARTH'S SURFACE

In this case $E = S$ and, as we saw in Chapter 3, the average temperature of the earth would be $-23\,°C$.

Case B *Earth with normal atmosphere*

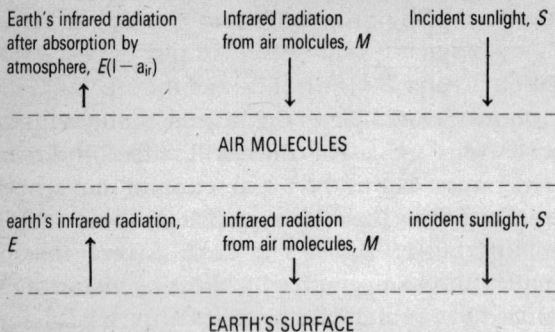

Earth's infrared radiation after absorption by atmosphere, $E(1 - a_{ir})$ ↑	Infrared radiation from air molcules, M ↓	Incident sunlight, S ↓

- -

AIR MOLECULES

- -

earth's infrared radiation, E ↑	infrared radiation from air molecules, M ↓	incident sunlight, S ↓

- -

EARTH'S SURFACE

Here I assume that a fraction a_{ir} of the earth's infrared radiation is absorbed by air molecules. Then equating the upward and downward flow of radiation at each level tells us that

$$S = M + E(1 - a_{ir})$$

and $E = S + M$

so the normal (average) amount of radiation emitted by the earth is

$$E_{normal} = \frac{2S}{2 - a_{ir}} \qquad [1]$$

The factor $2/(2 - a_{ir})$ which is now multiplying S, and which is always greater than 1, is the 'greenhouse' factor. In Chapter 3 we saw that the earth's average temperature is 13 °C and that the earth therefore radiates 70 per cent more energy than it receives from the sun, on average, so $E/S = 1.7$, and we need $a_{ir} = 0.82$ in equation [1]. This is a rather higher fraction of the earth's infrared radiation than the atmosphere is actually believed to absorb (about 70 per cent), but this is just because of the crudeness of the calculation.

Case C   Effect of veil of scattering particles (dust)

It is only those particles that scatter sunlight upwards away from the earth that will affect the ground temperature. Let a_{sc} be the fraction of sunlight scattered upwards. Then S in equation [1] above should be replaced by $(1 - a_{sc}) S$. The earth's average absolute temperature (temperature in °C + 273) would then be reduced by $(1 - a_{sc})^{1/4}$, or by 71 a_{sc} °C for small values of a_{sc}.

This case is relevant to volcanic dust veils, which are effective scatterers but poor absorbers of visible radiation. We saw that the Tambora volcanic dust-veil may have reduced the average ground temperature by as much as 3 °C in the lost summer of 1816 and this would require a_{sc} to be about 0.04. On the other hand the direct dimming of sunlight was estimated to have been by as much as 75 per cent (p.11). Taken together these two figures mean that the particles in the volcanic dust-veil must have mainly scattered the sunlight downwards. This is consistent with what is known about the properties of volcanic dust particles.

For the same reason the cooling effect of the dust generated in a nuclear war is likely to be small, as was found by the TTAPS scientists.

Case D   Atmosphere permeated with smoke (scattering neglected)

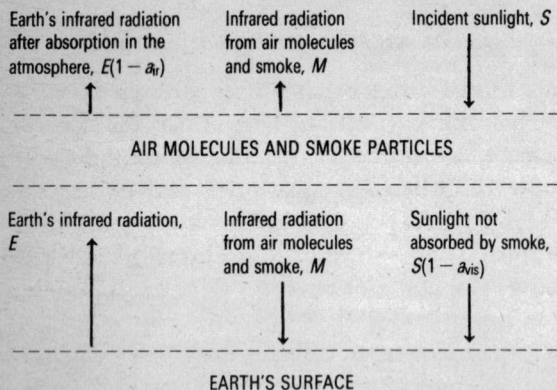

Earth's infrared radiation after absorption in the atmosphere, $E(1 - a_{ir})$ ↑	Infrared radiation from air molecules and smoke, M ↑	Incident sunlight, S ↓

AIR MOLECULES AND SMOKE PARTICLES

Earth's infrared radiation, E ↑	Infrared radiation from air molecules and smoke, M ↓	Sunlight not absorbed by smoke, $S(1 - a_{vis})$ ↓

EARTH'S SURFACE

Here a_{vis} is the fraction of the incident sunlight which is absorbed by smoke.

Then equating the upward and downward flow of radiation at each level:

$$S = M + E(1 - a_{ir})$$

and $$E = M + S(1 - a_{vis})$$

so $$E = \frac{S(2 - a_{vis})}{2 - a_{ir}} = E_{normal}\,(1 - a_{vis}/2).$$

The resulting temperature drop, compared with normal conditions, is shown in Table 1 (p.112) for different values of a_{vis}. Note that even if a_{vis} becomes 1, so that no visible light is transmitted through the smoke, E is still 50 per cent of normal, corresponding to a maximum temperature drop of 46 °C. Note also that if there are absorbing particles in the atmosphere, there is always a cooling.

Case E   Smoke cloud lying above most of the atmosphere

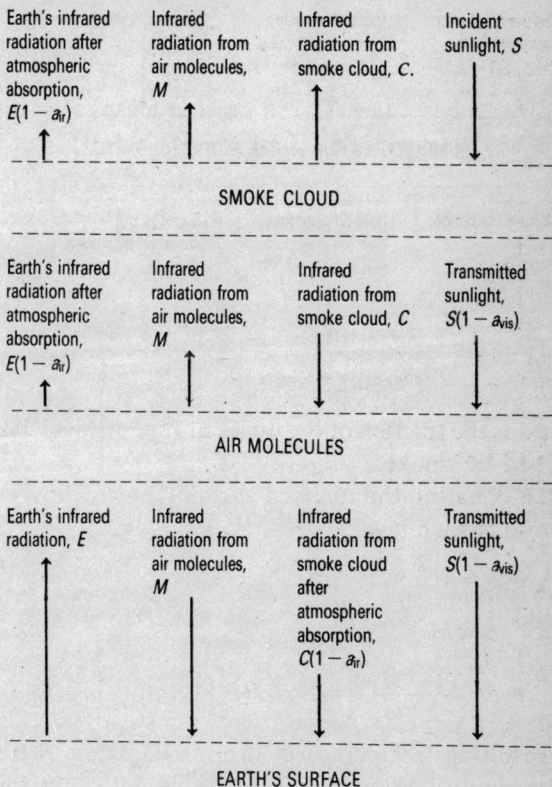

| Earth's infrared radiation after atmospheric absorption, $E(1 - a_{ir})$ ↑ | Infrared radiation from air molecules, M ↑ | Infrared radiation from smoke cloud, C. ↑ | Incident sunlight, S ↓ |

- -

SMOKE CLOUD

- -

| Earth's infrared radiation after atmospheric absorption, $E(1 - a_{ir})$ ↑ | Infrared radiation from air molecules, M ↑ | Infrared radiation from smoke cloud, C ↓ | Transmitted sunlight, $S(1 - a_{vis})$ ↓ |

- -

AIR MOLECULES

- -

| Earth's infrared radiation, E ↑ | Infrared radiation from air molecules, M ↓ | Infrared radiation from smoke cloud after atmospheric absorption, $C(1 - a_{ir})$ ↓ | Transmitted sunlight, $S(1 - a_{vis})$ ↓ |

- -

EARTH'S SURFACE

Equating the upward and downward flow of radiation at each level:

$$S = C + M + E(1 - a_{ir})$$

$$C + S(1 - a_{vis}) = M + E(1 - a_{ir})$$

and $\quad E = M + C(1 - a_{ir}) + S(1 - a_{vis})$.

Eliminating C and M, $E = \dfrac{S(-a_{vis} - a_{vis} a_{ir}/2)}{2 - a_{ir}}$

$$= E_{normal}(1 - a_{vis}/2 - a_{vis} a_{ir}/4)$$

Note that the last term in the bracket means that this case is always cooler than Case D (see Table 1).

Case F   Smoke cloud lying below most of the atmosphere

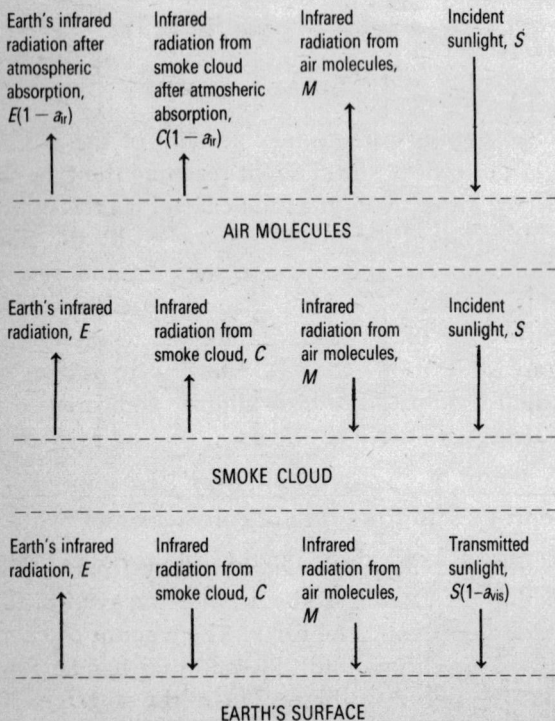

| Earth's infrared radiation after atmospheric absorption, $E(1 - a_{ir})$ | Infrared radiation from smoke cloud after atmosheric absorption, $C(1 - a_{ir})$ | Infrared radiation from air molecules, M | Incident sunlight, S |

AIR MOLECULES

| Earth's infrared radiation, E | Infrared radiation from smoke cloud, C | Infrared radiation from air molecules, M | Incident sunlight, S |

SMOKE CLOUD

| Earth's infrared radiation, E | Infrared radiation from smoke cloud, C | Infrared radiation from air molecules, M | Transmitted sunlight, $S(1 - a_{vis})$ |

EARTH'S SURFACE

Equating the upward and downward flow of radiation at each level:

$$S = M + C(1 - a_{ir}) + E(1 - a_{ir})$$

$$S + M = C + E$$

$$S(1 - a_{vis}) + M + C = E$$

so $E = \dfrac{S(2 - a_{vis} + a_{vis}\, a_{ir}/2)}{2 - a_{ir}} = E_{normal}\left(1 - a_{vis}/2 + a_{vis}\, a_{ir}/4\right).$

The last term in the bracket means that the temperature drop is always less than Case D, but there is still always a temperature drop (see Table 1).

The earth's albedo

It is straightforward to take account of the fact that 10–15 per cent of the sunlight reaching the ground is reflected away again. If a smoke cloud is present some of this reflected light will be absorbed by the cloud. Because of this and because some of the sunlight normally lost to the earth due to reflection is now absorbed by the smoke and radiated to the earth as infrared radiation, the net effect is to reduce the predicted temperature drop slightly compared to the predictions of Table 1.

The tropics and the role of convection of heat

On the equator the amount of energy from sunlight reaching the ground is about twice the average for a general location on the earth. The amount of energy radiated by the ground, on the other hand, is only about 20 per cent higher than the average. The difference between the two is made up by a strong upward convection by heat, which drives the Hadley cell circulation mentioned in Chapter 3.

If the sunlight is absorbed by a nuclear cloud of smoke, the most likely outcome is simply a reduction of the upward convection with no reduction of the ground temperature. In fact 80 per cent of the sunlight could be absorbed before the ground temperature would have to fall. Even if all the sunlight were to be absorbed $(a_{vis} = 1)$, the ground temperature at the equator would not need to fall below the earth's normal average temperature (13 °C).

However, although the cooling at the equator may not be too severe in a nuclear winter, the suppression of the vertical convection at the equator will lead to enhanced cooling at higher latitudes.

Table 1 Temperature drop as a function of a_{vis}, the fraction of sunlight absorbed by smoke

	a_{vis}					
	0.39	0.63	0.865	0.95	0.98	1
Case D (smoke permeates atmosphere (°C)	−14	−26	−38	−43	−45	−46
	−24	−39	−59	−69	−72	−75
Case E (smoke high) (°C)	−9	−14	−21	−23	−24	−24

Note: All the calculations given in this Appendix are very approximate, but they illustrate that an inevitable consequence of a strongly absorbing nuclear smoke cloud which covers much of the earth is a severe reduction in the ground temperature.

Further Reading

L. W. Alvarez, W. Alvarez, F. Asaro, H. V. Michel, Extraterrestial cause for the Cretaceous-Tertiary extinction, *Science* **208**, 1095 (1980)

H. A. Bethe, R. L. Garwin, K. Gottfried, H. W. Kendall, Space-based ballistic-missile defense, *Scientific American*, Oct. 1984, p.37

C. Covey, The earth's orbit and the ice ages, *Scientific American* Feb. 1984, p.42

C. Covey, S. H. Schneider, S. L. Thompson, Global effects of massive smoke injections from a nuclear war, *Nature* **308**, 21 (1984)

P. R. Ehrlich *et al.*, Long-term biological consequences of nuclear war, *Science* **222**, 1293 (1983)

P. R. Ehrlich, C. Sagan, D. Kennedy, W. O. Roberts, *The Cold and the Dark*. Sidgwick and Jackson 1984

O. Greene, I. Percival, I. Ridge, *The Nuclear Winter*. Blackwells (Polity) 1985

O. Greene, B. Rubin, N. Turok, P. Webber, G. Wilkinson, *London After the Bomb*, Oxford University Press 1982

Home Office Publications: *Protect and Survive* 1980; *Domestic Nuclear Shelters* 1981; *Nuclear Weapons* 1982

R. Jungk, *Brighter Than a Thousand Suns*. Pelican 1958

H. Kahn, *On Thermonuclear War*. Princeton University Press 1960

J. Maddox, Nuclear winter not yet established, *Nature* **308**, 11, (1984)

C. Meredith, O. Greene, M. Pentz, *Nuclear Winter*. SANA Publications 1984

M. R. Ramping and S. Self, The atmospheric effects of El Chichon, *Scientific American* Jan.1984, p.34

A. Rudolf, *Byron's 'Darkness': Lost Summer and Nuclear Winter*. Menard Press 1984

M. Ryle, *Towards the Nuclear Holocaust*. Menard Press 1980

C. Sagan, Nuclear war and climatic catastrophe: some policy implications, *Foreign Affairs* **62**, 257 (1984)

S. M. Stanley, Mass extinctions in the ocean, *Scientific American* June 1984, p.46

H. Stommel and E. Stommel, The year Without a summer, *Scientific American* June 1979, p.176

R. B. Stothers, The great Tambora eruption in 1815 and its Aftermath, *Science* **224**, 1191, (1984)

G. R. Taylor, *The Doomsday Book*. Thames and Hudson 1970

E. Teller, Widespread after-effects of nuclear war, *Nature* **310**, 621 (1984)

R. P. Turco, O. B. Toon, T. P. Ackerman, J. B. Pollack and C. Sagan (TTAPS), The climatic effects of nuclear war, *Scientific American* Aug. 1984, p.23

idem Nuclear winter: global consequences of multiple nuclear explosions, *Science* **222**, 1283, (1983)

US National Research Council, *The Effects on the Atmosphere of a Major Nuclear Exchange* 1985

Index

118